HOW
TO ENJOY
POETRY

HOW TO ENJOY POETRY

Vernon Scannell

Series Editor Melvyn Bragg

PIATKUS

First published in 1983 by Judy Piatkus (Publishers) Ltd of Loughton, Essex

Reprinted 1984

British Library Cataloguing in Publication Data

Scannell, Vernon
    How to enjoy poetry.—(Melvyn Bragg's arts series)
    1. Poetry
    1. Title   11. Series
    808.1   PN1031 . S3

    ISBN 0-86188-143-5

Designed by Zena Flax

Typeset by Phoenix Photosetting, Chatham
Printed and bound by Mackays of Chatham Ltd

contents

introduction

This book can be read with pleasure and profit by those who have the beginnings of an interest in poetry. As for those who know a lot, they cannot fail to be impressed by Vernon Scannell's lucid arguments. He is both approachable and authoritative. He touches on such questions as the essence of poetry and the origin of poetry; equally, he outlines a practical guide for those who might want to write their own. It is all done in an easy style, underpinned by unobtrusive scholarship.

Vernon Scannell has written a rare book in that it genuinely – and in my opinion, successfully – reaches out to help and instruct those who feel that they are at a disadvantage, while never being either patronising or simplistic. There are hundreds of thousands of people who like to write in verse, who enjoy the sound and fall of words, and yet who feel either too shy or nervous to ask the obvious questions which most intrigue them. What are the different rhyming schemes called and what can they do? How do you make words *sound* like their sense – galloping like 'Half a league, half a league, Half a league onward' or rallying like 'Once more unto the breach, dear friends, once more!' Tender, sensual, witty, emphatic – how can they sound like the feeling in your head? What, in the most particular and the grandest way, is poetry all about?

Poetry is a most wonderful art: to read, to listen to, to attempt. It takes the gift of language and pays it the respect of fashioning it into the finest forms while retaining a grip on the human-measure of life. For many, it is dinned into their unwilling heads at school, trailed across their noses in restless adolescence and ever after considered as part of 'another' world. Not the real, ordinary world. Yet the real world has been the poet's prime concern. And many of us believe that the real world has been represented more accurately and powerfully by poets than by anyone else. This book retains its sense of respect, but accepts the job of showing the craft, the history and the opportunities presented by poetry addressing the 'real' world.

Despite the constant cries of DOOM! DOOM!, the times and place we live in seem not too bad for poetry. Indeed, that would seem an over-cautious estimate when there are poets such as Hughes, Larkin and Heaney still at work; and scores of younger writers – Fenton, Longley, Raine, Muldoon et al – whose work is at least serious and at best might be lasting. For that is another, perhaps essential, attraction of poetry: its undoubted and proven power to communicate with posterity, to speak to the as-yet-unborn as easily as it enables us to be spoken to by the dead. It carries the messages of the generations. Perhaps that is one reason for the amazing response which meets any announcement of a poetry competition and the crowded reception an increasing number of poets now receive at readings and literary festivals.

When the idea for this series was first discussed, I was worried on several counts: one above all. Could a book be written of sufficient seriousness and commitment which would at the same time be available to that large number of enthusiastic but relatively uninformed people whose education or personal pace of development had caused them to miss out on 'the basics'? Vernon Scannell's book came as a great relief and a total justification for this enterprise. It will, I believe, help you to enjoy poetry in the widest sense – to understand it, appreciate it and wonder at it all the more.

Melvyn Bragg

9th November, 1982

1

WHAT
IS
POETRY?

The question 'What is poetry?' would seem to be a very simple one but in fact it has never been satisfactorily answered, although men and women of formidable intellect, from Aristotle to the present day, have attempted to provide their definitions. When Dr Johnson was asked this question he replied, 'Why, Sir, it is much easier to say what it is not. We all *know* what light is; but it is not easy to *tell* what it is.' Here the great poet, critic and lexicographer is suggesting that we immediately recognise poetry through our senses and that it can be defined only negatively, by presenting examples of writing which clearly lack the quality of poetry. He is probably right. My own favourite definition is the one which was dear to Robert Frost, the American poet, who said that poetry is that which gets left out when a poem is translated into another language.

Poetry is a special way of using words, and any interference with the selection and order of those words will destroy it. When we write prose we are primarily concerned with imparting information. The order of those words, even the words themselves, may be changed without any serious loss of efficacy. For example, in the sentence before the last, I could have written 'The prose-writer's chief concern is with communicating information', and the reader would have found the sentence more or less as acceptable as, and no different in meaning from, what I actually wrote. But if we tamper even slightly with the syntax and vocabulary of poetry the result will always be disastrous. Here is a verse from a poem by the Elizabethan, Thomas Nashe, who was writing during an outbreak of plague:

> Beauty is but a flower,
> Which wrinkles will devour,
> Brightness falls from the air,
> Queens have died young and fair,
> Dust hath closed Helen's eye.
> I am sick, I must die:
> Lord, have mercy on us.

A prose paraphrase of these lines would run something like this: 'Beauty is frail and will wither like a flower. It is getting dark. Young and beautiful queens have met premature deaths. Helen of Troy is dead. I am ill and I shall certainly die. God help us.'

Clearly the prose version, which has omitted nothing of the *sense* of the original, has lost all of the haunting beauty of the poetry. So, for practical purposes, we could say that poetry is a kind of writing which is unparaphrasable, untranslatable; its primary purpose is not to communicate information, but to induce in the reader or listener feelings as close as possible to those which have moved the poet to write. Its purpose is not to inform but to inflame. It is less interested in telling us *about* a thing than in presenting the thing itself.

The lines by Nashe (from *Summer's Last Will and Testament*) are written in a regular metre and rhyme, but this is not to say that all poetry must employ these devices, nor that all pieces of writing that do employ them are necessarily poetry. The bits of doggerel verse which appear in the In Memoriam columns of newspapers or on greeting cards make crude use of metre and rhyme, but to call them poems would be patently absurd. Conversely, the unfakeable resonances of genuine poetry are to be found in certain kinds of prose, in for instance the *Song of Solomon*, the *Book of Common Prayer*, in the majestic and unparaphrasable Sermons of John Donne, certain novels like James Joyce's *Ulysses* or Virginia Woolf's *To The Lighthouse*, and in this meditation from Herman Melville's novel *Moby Dick*:

> Nevertheless the sun hides not Virginia's Dismal
> Swamp, nor Rome's accursed Campagna, nor wide
> Sahara, nor all the millions of miles of deserts and of
> griefs beneath the moon. The sun hides not the ocean,
> which is the dark side of this earth, and which is two
> thirds of this earth. So, therefore, that mortal man who
> hath more of joy than sorrow in him, that mortal man
> cannot be true – not true, or undeveloped. With books
> the same. The truest of all men was the Man of
> Sorrows, and the truest of all books is Solomon's, and
> Ecclesiastes is the fine hammered steel of woe. All is
> vanity. ALL. This wilful world hath not got hold of
> unchristian Solomon's wisdom yet. But he who dodges
> hospitals and jails, and walks fast crossing graveyards,
> and would rather talk of operas than hell; calls
> Cowper, Young, Pascal, Rousseau, poor devils all of
> sick men; and throughout a carefree lifetime swears
> by Rabelais as passing wise, and therefore jolly:- not
> that man is fitted to sit down on tomb stones, and
> break the green damp mould with unfathomably
> wondrous Solomon.

Poetry, then, is first a matter of using language with the greatest possible precision, evocativeness and sonority in order to convey emotion through the presentation of things; it is sensuous, passionate and penetrating. For the poet, words are not simply ciphers whose sole function is to communicate abstract meanings; they are not static counters but living, changing things, each with its own colour, texture, weight and flavour. What the poem says in the paraphrasable sense, its 'meaning', is often not very important. The pleasure we derive from poetry is not greatly dissimilar from the pleasure given by music. A Chopin Prelude, a Beethoven Quartet or, for that matter, a simple dance tune or march do not tell us anything;

they are unlikely to change our philosophical, political or religious opinions. They may exhilarate, or stir in us a pleasant melancholy, a serene joy, or even ecstatic affirmation of the glory and splendour of being alive. We do not ask what the melody means, any more than we would ask the meaning of a daffodil or a tree. This is essentially true of poetry, too, though since poems are made of words, and words by definition possess meaning, the situation is rather more complex. There are literary critics who have maintained that it is as illegitimate to ask what a poem means as it would be to ask the same of a musical composition. But I am sure that they are wrong in adopting this attitude to poetry. The meaning, or subject matter, of a poem is important, but principally because it has prompted the poet to express it in a particular way. At the risk of over-simplifying I should say that poetry is *how* the thing is said rather than *what* is said. Let me give a simple illustration. Here is a short poem by Thomas Hardy:

> I look into my glass,
> And view my wasting skin,
> And say, 'Would God it came to pass
> My heart had shrunk as thin!'
>
> For then, I, undistrest
> By hearts grown cold to me,
> Could lonely wait my endless rest
> With equanimity.
>
> But Time, to make me grieve,
> Part steals, lets part abide;
> And shakes this fragile frame at eve
> With throbbings of noontide.

Now these lines do not tell us anything we did not already know. The 'meaning' is simple almost to the point of banality. An old person looks into a mirror at the lines and wrinkles of old age, and thinks how painfully difficult it is to reconcile the physical processes of ageing with the fact that the heart and its affections remain unchanged, eager and vulnerable as in youth. The poignancy is a result, not of the message, but of the way in which it is presented. Hardy does not generalise or make abstract statements about the condition of growing old. He presents a specific situation through the deployment of physical images. The ageing person looks into an actual glass and sees the physical reality of 'wasting skin'. The exclamation, 'Would God it came to pass/My heart had shrunk as thin', is wrung from him by the shock of confrontation with age and mortality; it is a true *cri de coeur*. The second line in the next stanza contains a phrase which I believe to be deliberately and fruitfully ambiguous. When Hardy speaks of 'hearts grown cold to me' he means that, if his own heart had withered like his flesh, he would be quite indifferent to the betrayals, to the death of love in the hearts of those who once cared for him; but, in juxtaposition to 'my endless rest', it could also mean those hearts that have grown cold in the grave, the dead whom once he had loved. The rhythm and verbal music add significantly to the total effect, especially in the last stanza when the repetitions of the initial sounds in 'fragile', 'frame' and 'throb' create a physical vibration that disquietingly echoes the sense.

The poem is a short, meditative lyric of a kind that is quite common in the work of Hardy and in English poetry itself, but of course it is not the only kind of poetry and other kinds offer different pleasures. When I hear people say that they do not care for poetry I wonder if they realise exactly what it is they are saying. They are professing indifference to the great treasury of anonymous ballads from the fifteenth century, poems that were learnt by heart and handed down from generation to generation, tales in vigorous rhymed verse, sad, macabre, violent and funny, a tradition which has been continued into our own times. They are rejecting the great epics recounting deeds of heroism and high adventure, the witty satires attacking institutions, persons, ideologies, abuses and follies with the deflating arrows of ridicule; poetic drama, the mighty plays of the Elizabethans and Jacobeans, Marlowe, Webster, Jonson and Shakespeare himself. They are unmoved by comic verses whose purpose it is simply to make us laugh, elegiac poems that move us to tears; devotional poetry praising God, erotic poetry praising the flesh and the vagaries of human love; poetry of war, poetry of peace, poetry celebrating nature and human nature; philosophical poetry and the magical verse of incantation. The man or woman who is indifferent to poetry is confessing to being indifferent to language, to what, in fact, separates humanity from the lower animals; ultimately it is a rejection of life itself. But it is my firm belief that there are few people who are unmoved by poetry, though there are many who believe themselves to be. There are many reasons for this.

Among the prejudices against the art of poetry is the misguided notion that it is a precious activity practised and enjoyed only by highly educated, other-worldly and doubtfully masculine intellectuals. This view of the poet as a cissy, or a zany eccentric, is one which seems to have been born towards the end of the nineteenth century; before that time it would have been incomprehensible. Certainly during the reign of the first Queen Elizabeth the man who could not write a gracefully turned poem to his mistress's charms as readily as he could use his sword in defence of her honour would not be regarded as a complete man. The history of English poetry is filled with the names of fine practitioners of the art who were also distinguished soldiers, sailors, men of action: Chaucer, Sidney, Wyatt, Raleigh, Marlowe, Jonson, the Cavalier Poets, Byron and our twentieth-century poets of the two World Wars. The notion that poets were creatures that took refuge from the rough and tumble of ordinary existence in their ivory towers, where they penned exquisite meditations on Truth and Beauty, was fostered by that period of English art and letters in the 1890s known as the *fin de siècle* or Decadence. In fact it was a time when very little English poetry of great and lasting value was produced, though unfortunately it did much to establish the figure of the artist and poet in the public imagination as someone apart from the common run of humanity, morally suspect and quite probably insane. The facts are quite otherwise.

The poet, as Wordsworth said, is a man speaking to men, and poetry has its roots firmly planted in the soil of common human experience and common speech. There is an impulse towards poetry at the heart of ordinary language, an instinctive tendency to make images, so we are often responding to a kind of poetry when we are not conscious of doing so. People's fondness of puns – to hear them or to make them – reveals an elementary need for poetry. The idioms of common speech are filled with metaphors, many of them striking and vigorous. 'It's bucketing down,' someone will observe on a rainy day, and they will be using language poetically. The word 'bucket' is a noun, but it is used here as a verb, and it is an impressive example of linguistic compression: the speaker means that the rain is coming down so heavily that it seems to be poured from buckets – he has compressed fifteen words down to three.

Another widely held misconception is that poetry – especially modern poetry – is 'difficult' or 'obscure'. It is quite easy to see how this belief has taken root and it is one I can sympathise with, for, if the general reader were to pick up an anthology or magazine of contemporary verse, he might well find poem-shaped patterns of words on the page that would yield, quite literally, neither rhyme nor reason. The regrettable truth is that, in the case of poetry, as with the other arts, a good deal of rubbish manages to get itself accepted and publicised by promoters who try to compensate for lack of judgement by substituting a blind confidence in fashionable novelty. Nevertheless the problem of poetic obscurity is a real one, and it is by no means peculiar to the twentieth century. Not all poets who have been accused of obscurity are charlatans. Keats, Shelley, Tennyson and Browning were all regarded by some of their contemporary readers as impenetrably difficult. The reason why some genuine poetry is labelled 'obscure' or 'meaningless' is often because the reader has approached it in the wrong way. He has come to it with preconceived ideas of what it should offer him and, when these expectations are disappointed, he turns away in bafflement, probably with the strong suspicion that he is being cheated.

Someone who has read widely in, say, eighteenth- and nineteenth-century poetry, but knows nothing of work written in our own time, would probably be even more perplexed by T. S. Eliot's *The Waste Land* or some of Dylan Thomas's lyrics than one who has read no poetry whatever and consequently has no precise expectations to be denied. Some poems, and the two examples I have quoted are of this kind, do offer the reader 'meaning' in the sense that a piece of plain prose contains meaning, though, as I hope I have shown, they do far more than this. But there are poems, particularly of the twentieth century, which are not concerned with meaning in the discursive prose sense at all. This type of poem may be composed of a series of 'images' which are emotionally inter-related, and no statement about their inter-relation is provided by the poet. We should not ask of such works, 'What does the poet mean? What is his message?', but simply surrender to the sound and the sequence of sensory images which unfolds before us – though later, perhaps after a number of readings, we may wish to supply our own interpretation, and attribute to the poem a 'meaning' which the poet quite deliberately has refrained from supplying.

Here is a little-known but, for me, very attractive lyrical poem by Charles Dalmon:

> O what if the fowler my blackbird has taken?
> The roses of dawn blossom over the sea;
> Awaken, my blackbird, awaken, awaken,
> And sing to me out of my red fuchsia tree!
>
> O what if the fowler my blackbird has taken?
> The sun lifts his head from the lap of the sea –
> Awaken, my blackbird, awaken, awaken,
> And sing to me out of my red fuchsia tree!
>
> O what if the fowler my blackbird has taken?
> The mountan grows white with the birds of the sea;
> But down in my garden, forsaken, forsaken,
> I'll weep all the day by my red fuchsia tree!

When I first came across this poem many years ago I read it with great pleasure, enjoying the rise and fall of the rhythms which seemed to reflect the undulations of the waves of the sea. I enjoyed the colours, the contrasts of the glossy black plumage of the bird, the misty rose and the dramatic red fuchsia, and I enjoyed the mellifluous combinations of echoing vowels and consonants, but I had no clear idea of what the poem was about, nor did I care. The rhythms and images communicated, effectively for me, a sense of the threat of losing something inestimably valuable. The lack of prose meaning, of plot, of explanation, far from being an obstacle to enjoyment, was part of the poem's attractiveness. If pressed, I might perhaps say that it is a love poem, that the blackbird is an emblem of the poet's love, which he desperately fears to lose, and that the fowler represents death. At another time, depending on my own circumstances and emotional or imaginative needs, I might decide that the blackbird is the poet's talent, the mysterious gift of song, deprived of which he would be disconsolate, and that the fowler is a symbol of the hostile forces of materialism, the predator, the killer. And if the author were to say, 'But I had no ideas of that kind at all when I wrote the poem', I should not be in the least disconcerted, for poetry of this kind, through its lack of explicit meaning, possesses almost inexhaustible possible meanings.

There is one final prejudice against poetry which can easily be disposed of: it is the fairly popular belief, closely related to the notion of the poet as inhabitant of the ivory tower or sacred grove, that he or she finds inspiration only in experiences of an elevated, even ethereal nature, that the poet fastidiously withdraws from the ordinary business of everyday living and loving and is concerned only with creating an alternative, idealised world from which the brute realities of existence are eliminated. Such poets and such poetry have indeed existed, but they are exceptional, especially in Britain. If we look only at the range of English love poetry we shall find every strand of the elaborate and contradictory fabric of erotic passion explored: we shall encounter poems which idealise all the attributes of the beloved, but also those which record her imperfections; poems which express the anguish of unrequited love, of rejection, of jealousy and despair. There is also a steady tradition of a poetry which celebrates the glory and absurdity, the comedy and delight of simple physical love, a tradition stretching from Chaucer to Robert Graves. Here, for instance, is a little poem by John Wilmot, Earl of Rochester (1647–1680) which is as outspoken about sexuality as any post-*Chatterley* novelist, yet is imbued with both wit and true tenderness:

A SONG
Of a Young LADY
To Her Ancient Lover

Ancient Person, for whom I
All the flattering Youth defie,
Long it be e'er thou grow Old
Aching, shaking, crazy, cold.
But still continue as thou art,
Ancient Person of my Heart.

On thy withered Lips and dry,
Which like barren Furrows lie,
Brooding Kisses I will pour,
Shall thy youthful Heat restore.
Such kind showers in Autumn fall,
And a second Spring recall:
Nor from thee will ever part,
Ancient Person of my Heart.

Thy Nobler Parts, which but to name
In our Sex would be counted shame,
By Age's frozen Grasp possessed
From their Ice shall be released:
And, soothed by my reviving Hand,
In former Warmth and Vigour stand.
All a Lover's Wish can reach
For thy Joy my Love shall teach:
And for thy Pleasure shall improve
All that Art can add to Love.
Yet still I love thee without Art,
Ancient Person of my Heart.

I hope that in this short chapter I have been able to convey to the reader some indication of the immense range of subject matter, tone and style to be found in the poetry of the English language, and perhaps to dispel a few of the prejudices that stand in the way of the enjoyment of poetry. I am convinced that any literate person, with a little patience and concentration and the willingness to submit to the power of poetic language and the poetic vision, will be able – given some guidance – to discover in the experience of reading poetry delight, excitement, enrichment and consolation of a kind that no other art form can provide. In the following pages I shall do my best to supply that necessary guidance.

2

APPRECIATING POETRY

When an author addresses himself to the writing of a poem he is doing something quite different from when he sits down to write a piece of prose. Broadly speaking, the prose-writer has a fairly clear idea in his mind of what it is he wishes to say, and he can judge the ultimate success of his finished work by the degree to which it corresponds to the ideal composition which existed in his head before he put pen to paper or fingertips to typewriter keys. This is unlikely to be true for a poet. Usually a poem has its origin in an experience that has, in some way, been important to the writer. The experience may be one in which he has been directly involved, or it may be one that he has witnessed as an impartial viewer, or merely one about which he has read or been told. It might be a large-scale dramatic event like a natural or artificial disaster, a violent accident, a cataclysmic storm or a display of human violence, individual or collective; it could be a private experience like falling in or out of love, or being savaged by grief through the death or dereliction of one close to the writer's heart, or it could be something as perfectly simple as being moved to joy or sorrow by a caprice of the weather, a whim of light, a scent or tune evoking a distant memory of childhood. Whatever the starting-point, when he begins the act of composition, the writer usually has no very clear idea of what direction the poem will take, and he may well finish with a conclusion that surprises himself.

If this is true – and with some slight qualification regarding long philosophical poems such as Wordsworth's *The Prelude* or didactic poems like Pope's *Essay on Criticism* I believe it to be irrefutably so – then making a poem is a far more exploratory act than writing prose. Where the prose-writer sets down his preconceived conclusions upon experience, where he records and analyses his findings, the poet, taking the tools of language and poetic technique (and the next chapter will be, in part, a kit-inspection of these) explores the experience; the writing of a poem is a voyage of discovery. As Robert Frost has written: 'It [the poem] has an outcome that though unforeseen was predestined from the first image of the original mood and indeed from the very mood.'

Perhaps I can make this more clear by using a poem of my own which will serve as a particular example of what I have been discussing in general terms:

A Case of Murder

They should not have left him there alone,
Alone that is except for the cat.
He was only nine, not old enough
To be left alone in a basement flat,
Alone, that is, except for the cat.
A dog would have been a different thing,
A big gruff dog with slashing jaws,
But a cat with round eyes mad as gold,
Plump as a cushion with tucked-in paws –
Better have left him with a fair-sized rat!
But what they did was leave him with a cat.
He hated that cat; he watched it sit,
A buzzing machine of soft black stuff,
He sat and watched and he hated it,
Snug in its fur, hot blood in a muff,
And its mad gold stare and the way it sat
Crooning dark warmth: he loathed all that.
So he took Daddy's stick and he hit the cat.

Then quick as a sudden crack in glass
It hissed, black flash, to a hiding place
In the dust and dark beneath the couch,
And he followed the grin on his new-made face,
A wide-eyed, frightened snarl of a grin,
And he took the stick and he thrust it in,
Hard and quick in the furry dark.
The black fur squealed and he felt his skin
Prickle with sparks of dry delight.
Then the cat again came into sight,
Shot for the door that wasn't quite shut,
But the boy, quick too, slammed fast the door:
The cat, half-through, was cracked like a nut
And the soft black thud was dumped on the floor.
Then the boy was suddenly terrified
And he bit his knuckles and cried and cried;
But he had to do something with the dead thing there.
His eyes squeezed beads of salty prayer
But the wound of fear gaped wide and raw;
He dared not touch the thing with his hands
So he fetched a spade and shovelled it
And dumped the load of heavy fur
In the spidery cupboard under the stair
Where it's been for years, and though it died
It's grown in that cupboard and its hot low purr
Grows slowly louder year by year:
There'll not be a corner for the boy to hide
When the cupboard swells and all sides split
And the huge black cat pads out of it.

The factual starting-point of this poem was an encounter with
an acquaintance who told me that, when he and his wife had
been out on a shopping expedition, they had returned home to
find their nine-year-old son in a deeply distressed condition.
At first the boy would not, or could not, say what was troubling
him, but finally he confessed to his mother that while they had
been out of the house, he had 'accidentally killed the cat'.
Apparently the parents did not at that point press him for
details, being more concerned with easing his seriously over-
wrought condition, so I knew no more then, nor did I subsequently find out any more, than that somehow the child had
'accidentally killed the cat'.

Now this incident occurred many years ago, in the

early 1960s, at a time when I was reading an extraordinary book by the psychoanalyst Bruno Bettelheim, called *The Informed Heart*; it was a study, partly autobiographical, for the author had been a prisoner in Belsen, of SS methods employed in the Nazi concentration camps. Bettelheim's book contained many horrifying instances of the brutality and sadism practised by the camp guards, so the poem was written at a time when I was much haunted and perplexed by the blood-freezing capacity of men to inflict appalling suffering on other men, and by the nature of sadism, remorse and guilt. The small boy's killing of the cat was linked to those preoccupations, but I am quite sure that I had no *conscious* intention of exploring them in the poem. All I started with was the disturbing fact that the child, left on his own with a cat, had somehow contrived to kill it. How could this have happened?

When I began to write I was concerned only with the physical details. The first two lines, with their emphatic, rather childish rhythm, suggested the shape the rest of the piece should take. I transferred the incident from a house to a flat partly to add to the claustrophobic feeling, but also because I felt that those childlike rhymes of 'cat', 'rat', 'sat', seemed appropriately elementary, redolent of the nursery, that their innocent simplicity would hint at the childishness of the protagonist but, at the same time, reinforce the very unchildlike, uninnocent nature of what was to come.

I had not the least idea of how the poem would proceed, except that the cat was to be killed, nor of how it would end. To a very large extent I allowed the movement of the rhythm and the images that it engendered to dictate the course of the narrative. The events depicted are quite realistic until the cat is being killed and the child is overcome by horror and remorse for his deed. Clearly, the poem takes on another dimension when the cat has been hidden in the cupboard: it moves away from realism into the realm of nightmare, the symbolic or allegorical.

Various readers have interpreted the ending in different ways. One man once congratulated me on writing an effective poem about Black Power. I certainly had no intention of writing about racial conflict, but I can see that it might be interpreted as such. The point is that, since I had myself no

preconceived idea of how the piece would develop and conclude, I surprised myself by the ending and, having written it,
had to ask myself what I meant by it. I believe that it pro-
ceeded from my own preoccupations with 'man's inhumanity
to man', and that the poem explores to some extent the nature
of sadism, violence, repression and guilt. Provided that the
reader does not actually misread the poem, that is, miscon-
strue the literal meaning – and it would surely be very difficult
to do so – then he is free to attribute whatever significance he
wishes to the symbolic or allegorical elements in the writing.

If, then, it is accepted that the writing of poetry is
essentially different from the writing of prose, it follows that
the reading of it is also an activity that involves a different
approach. When we read prose, whether it is plain factual
writing of a didactic or polemical nature such as a newspaper
editorial, or the narrative of history and biography or fiction
(though some qualification is required here), a single attentive
reading will yield the substance that the writer has been concerned with communicating. It is true that one can derive
pleasure from the rhythms, the phrasing, the radiance and
eloquence of excellent prose, but these are a secondary
pleasure, a means to the end of effectively imparting information, describing character, scene or action, advancing the
narrative. It is only very rarely that a single reading of a poem
will discover all that the work has to offer.

I am aware that this may sound forbidding. The reader
may well, and understandably, say, 'I read for pleasure,
relaxation, entertainment. I don't want reading to become a
labour, a demanding task. That's all right for professionals, for
academics and critics and so on, but not for me.' I suggest,
though, that the rewards we can receive from reading poetry
more than repay the efforts expended. Reading for relaxation, for temporary escape from the problems of everyday
existence, the effortless swallowing of thrillers, romances,
light biography and so on is, of course, an enjoyable and perfectly legitimate indulgence and one which no one need feel
ashamed of enjoying. However, there is a crucial difference
between reading of this kind, this negative self-immersion in
fantasy, and the tougher but infinitely more satisfying and,
finally, infinitely more pleasurable activity of appreciating

true literature. Through the reading of authentic literature –
and poetry is its highest form – we can experience modes of
consciousness from which otherwise we would be totally
debarred, and our sympathies, our tolerance, our understanding of life itself may be immeasurably enriched. Let me give a
simple example of this.

For someone who is, for reasons of education, temperament, environment, or from logical conviction, more or
less without religious feeling, it is almost impossible to understand the nature of religious faith: the arguments of theolo-
gians and the dusty preaching of clerics are unlikely to be persuasive. Yet an acquaintance with the sonnets of Gerard Manley Hopkins, the Jesuit priest (1844–1899), which deal with his
sense of despair at a time when he was suffering what St John
of the Cross called 'the dark night of the soul' – the feeling of
separation from God – compels one to identify with the poet in
his mental anguish. We are not *told* what it is like to undergo
such an experience; we are compelled to *share* it. Conversely
we can experience the pure joy of religious certainty through
the devotional poems of George Herbert (1593–1633), as in
this sonnet called simply *Prayer*:

Prayer the Churches banquet, Angels age,
  Gods breath in man returning to his birth,
The soul in paraphrase, heart in pilgrimage,
  The christian plummet sounding heav'n and earth:

Engine against th'Almightie, sinners towre,
  Reversed thunder, Christ-side-piercing spear,
The six-daies world transposing in an houre,
  A kinde of tune, which all things heare and fear;

Softnesse, and peace, and joy, and love, and blisse,
  Exalted Manna, gladnesse of the best,
  Heaven in ordinarie, man well drest,
The milkie way, the bird of Paradise,

  Church-bells beyond the starres heard,
                the souls blood,
  The land of spices, something understood.

Using this little poem for the purposes of practical demonstration, we can now return to the essential difference between
reading prose and reading poetry. As I have said, one reading,
even with a comparatively simple poem like *Prayer*, will not
reveal its full riches. I have found that the best approach to
reading any poem is a three-stage one. With the first exploration of the poem the reader should not attempt to extract all
that the work contains; he should not stop to tease away at
any phrase or image that seems obscure or perplexing. But the
poem should be read more slowly than would a passage of
prose, so that the music of the verse is given time to expand
and assert its rhythm in the reader's consciousness. Although
we might not read the poem aloud in the literal, physical
sense, I believe that we should always *hear* the language as
we read, and that the pace of our reading should be no faster
than it would be if we were actually declaiming the verses
aloud to an audience.

A first reading, then, of *Prayer* should show the
reasonably attentive reader that the poem is a description and
a joyful celebration of the act of praying, expressing gratitude
for its gift and examining its supernatural nature. We should
have noticed, though perhaps not in close detail, the way in
which Herbert advances through a series of metaphors, most
of which seem to contain contradictory elements. Almost certainly we shall have been pleased by the way the poem concludes, after the sequence of elaborate and quite complex
images, with its very simple statement: 'something understood'. Now we should embark on the second reading.

This should proceed much more slowly, concentrating
on each word or group of words, each image. The opening
phrase, 'Prayer the Churches banquet...', suggests
immediately the festive and *nourishing* nature of prayer
which is both a banquet to which the Church invites members
and a feast which nourishes the mystical body of the Church
itself. 'Angels age ...' conveys the sense of immortality,
agelessness, as opposed to man's limited three score years
and ten, prayer being the expression of that part of man which
is indestructible and timeless, 'Gods breath in man'. The final
line of the first quatrain (a four-line verse) shows the use of an
apparently self-contradictory image to dramatise the poet's

meaning: the plummet, a lead ball attached to a line and used by builders to determine the vertical or to sound depths, is here reversed, reaching from earth up to heaven, and this reversal sets the pattern of the paradoxical images that follow. The 'engine' (line 5) carries the seventeenth-century meaning of 'missile, seige gun or catapult', which hurls the missile of prayer, the 'sinners toure' is prayer aspiring like a steeple to the heavens; prayer is conceived of as 'reversed thunder' which, unlike natural thunder, has its source on earth and is heard in the heavens. And so the paradoxical metaphors unfold until, in line 10, we find a conceit (see page 96) of extraordinary neatness and power when Herbert describes prayer as 'Exalted Manna', that is manna which, instead of descending from heaven, rises from earth back to its original divine source. The final lines counterpoint the mundane and commonplace against the exotic and universal.

Having completed the second detailed reading with a careful examination of the meaning or possible meanings, we should look at the structure of the poem and determine to what extent the form is appropriate to the mood and content expressed, and observe the slight changes in pace and rhythm, although the poem (an irregularly rhymed sonnet) is composed throughout in the same basic metre, the nature of which we shall be exploring in the next chapter. After this third look at the poem we should be ready to go back and enjoy it as a whole, savouring all its splendours, the sound, the interplay of sensations, the colours, the cleverness and deep feeling of the essential meaning.

One of the quickest and most enjoyable ways of acquiring the skill of reading poetry and fully responding to it is to listen to trained and gifted speakers of verse. During the past twenty years or so public performances of poets reading their own work have become regular features of almost all cultural festivals. Poets regularly visit schools, colleges and literary societies all over the country to read and to talk about their writing, and most of them have made it their business to acquire a suitable style of delivery which will communicate to an audience those qualities of sound, sense and structure that make their poems distinctive. Then there are other public recitals of a different kind, where the poetry spoken is presented by accomplished speakers of verse who are often well-known actors and actresses. Both kinds of spoken poetry exist in abundance on gramophone records and may be found in any public library which has a record department, and of course in any good gramophone record shop.

If you listen to a skilful speaker of verse you will notice that every word is clearly enunciated and that the rhythm of the poem is never blurred or lost, although it should not be over-emphasised to create an obtrusively thumping effect, and the cadences of normal speech should always be preserved. The inferior speaker – and I am afraid some quite well-known actors fall into this category – does not simply articulate the poem as he should, allowing the words and images to convey the emotion, but attempts to add further emotional and dramatic resonances by a histrionic delivery of the lines. The excellent speaker of verse recognises that the poem is not a means by which he can project his own personality, and display the beauty of his voice and his talents as an actor, but that it is a verbal construct which must be displayed with such clarity of voice and understanding of the poet's intentions as that actor may command.

The more first-rate poetry you read and listen to, the more discerning your taste will become, but here you may reasonably ask: 'How can I know what is first-rate from what is second-, third- or even tenth-rate?' Judgements of the relative merits of poems must ultimately be subjective and therefore, in the absolute scientific sense, their soundness cannot be proved. However, no one could possibly doubt that Keats's *Ode to a Nightingale*, for instance, is a better poem than T. E. Brown's *My Garden* (both to be found in the first *Oxford Book of English Verse* edited by Quiller-Couch) or that *Hamlet* or *King Lear* contain infinitely greater poetry than Christopher Fry's *The Lady's not for Burning*. Furthermore, I believe that it is demonstrably possible to distinguish between the excellent and the slightly flawed, taking two works by the same poet. Here, for example, are two poems by Wilfred Owen who, at the age of twenty-six, was killed in the First World War just one week before the Armistice in 1918:

Greater Love

Red lips are not so red
    As the stained stones kissed by the English dead.
Kindness of wooed and wooer
Seems shame to their love pure.
O Love, your eyes lose lure
    When I behold eyes blinded in my stead!

Your slender attitude
    Trembles not exquisite like limbs knife-skewed,
Rolling and rolling there
Where God seems not to care;
Till the fierce love they bear
    Cramps them in death's extreme decrepitude.

Your voice sings not so soft, –
    Though even as wind murmuring through
                        raftered loft,
Your dear voice is not dear,
Gentle, and evening clear,
As theirs whom none now hear,
    Now earth has stopped their piteous mouths
                        that coughed.

Heart, you were never hot
    Nor large, nor full like hearts made great with shot;
And though your hand be pale,
Paler are all which trail
Your cross through flame and hail:
    Weep, you may weep, for you may touch them not.

The Send-Off

Down the close, darkening lanes they sang their way
To the siding-shed,
And lined the train with faces grimly gay.

Their breasts were stuck all white with wreath
                        and spray
As men's are, dead.

Dull porters watched them, and a casual tramp
Stood staring hard,
Sorry to miss them from the upland camp.
Then, unmoved, signals nodded, and a lamp
Winked to the guard.

So secretly, like wrongs hushed-up, they went.
They were not ours:
We never heard to which front these were sent.

Nor there if they yet mock what women meant
Who gave them flowers.

Shall they return to beatings of great bells
In wild train-loads?
A few, a few, too few for drums and yells,
May creep back, silent, to still village wells
Up half-known roads.

First we should take *Greater Love* and read it slowly and carefully, straight through, in the way that I previously suggested.
This first reading gives me a sense of the poet's anguish and
guilt at being alive when his comrades have died horribly on
the battlefields. It seems that he is addressing a woman whom
he loves, and he contrasts the physical details of their loving
with those of the soldiers in their death throes. However, the
final stanza, with its reference to 'Your cross . . .' puzzled me,
for it seemed to suggest that he was here apostrophising
Christ. The second, more concentrated reading corrected this
impression: it becomes clear now that, though he is indeed
addressing a beloved woman, she is not only a specific person
but also a representative of womankind. The lines 'Paler are
all which trail/Your cross through flame and hail . . .' refer, I
think, to those who have sacrificed their lives for the women,
who are literally women, but could also symbolise home, the
Motherland, domestic certainties, peace.

A third examination of the poem, paying attention to
structure and form, confirmed what my ear had been rather
distressed by on the first reading: the repetition of the sibilant
in 'As the stained stones kissed by the English dead . . ' is

31

clumsily handled. It may well be that the poet wished to enact the sound of kissing onomatopoeically, but those repeated 's' sounds create an unfortunate hissing effect. The stanza form, with the varying line length, is resourcefully handled, but the rhymes 'wooer' and 'pure' strike my ear as inaccurate and dreadfully false. The juxtaposing of soft, sensuous language with harsh, staccato words – 'slender' . . . 'trembles' . . . 'limbs' . . . 'with knife-skewed' . . . – is, I am sure, deliberate, but the total effect is one of an ambiguity that I do not think the poet intended to convey. There is an uncomfortable sense of the poet almost revelling in the images of carnage, which are presented in terms of physical love and sexuality.

The Send-Off strikes me as a far more consistently satisfactory poem. Here the language is restrained and the poet shows a marked preference for the simplest rather than the most sonorous word. There are no troubling ambiguities in this poem. The troops in the evening march to the station from which they are to be transported to the Front. Some are wearing flowers which have been pinned on to them by the women who watch them march past. The tramp, who has no doubt received tit-bits from the cookhouse of their camp, seems the only bystander who is moved by their departure. The poet, obviously a soldier from another camp and unit – 'they were not ours' – speculates on their future, knowing that many will be killed and that the survivors will return, not to a hero's welcome, but to a sad, bereaved and almost alien place.

While Greater Love possesses some fine qualities, I would claim with some confidence that The Send-Off is the better poem. Where the first is straining to elicit a sense of the waste of war through generalisation and highly-coloured, dramatic language and images, The Send-Off deals with a particular event and does not attempt to extract from it, or to inject into it, more drama and emotional force than the situation actually contains. The second is the better poem because it is completely truthful. Here Owen does not try to bludgeon his reader into a shocked state of horror at the cruelties of war: he simply presents one simple scene, but one which contains in a muted way all the pathos of loss and futility that the First World War has come to symbolise for succeeding generations.

In examining the poems quoted in this chapter I have

deliberately avoided, as far as possible, the use of technical terms, so any comments on structure and technique have been necessarily superficial. In the next chapter we shall be taking a look at the ways in which the poet achieves his effects - inspecting, as it were, the tools of his trade – and in the process it will be necessary to acquaint ourselves with some of the vocabulary of poetic criticism. However, I shall do my best to simplify wherever possible, and avoid burdening the reader with terminology and theory that are not essential for full appreciation and understanding of the art of poetry.

3

THE POET'S CRAFT

The science of versification which embraces the laws of metre, the devices of rhyme, alliteration and assonance, is known as prosody. It is not necessary to have any knowledge of prosody in order to respond to poetry, any more than one must understand the principles of notation, harmony and counterpoint before music can be enjoyed; but, as with any art form, pleasure is considerably deepened by an understanding of the craftsmanship commanded by the artist. For anyone who wishes to write poetry, at least a basic grasp of the elements of prosody is absolutely necessary. As the American poet and critic Ezra Pound said, 'Don't imagine that the art of poetry is any simpler than the art of music. . . .'

It is a common error, and unfortunately one encouraged by some poets and teachers of literature, that poems are not carefully constructed artefacts but the spontaneous outpourings of men and women in a state of trance, emotional turmoil or demonic possession. In a letter to his publisher, John Taylor, written in February 1818, Keats said, 'If it comes not as naturally as leaves to a tree it had better not come at all', and Wordsworth, in his Preface to the *Lyrical Ballads*, made the much-quoted observation: 'Poetry is the spontaneous overflow of powerful feelings: it takes its origin from emotion recollected in tranquillity.' It is statements like these which have misled readers into believing that the act of composing is an automatic, mindless process. When both Keats and Wordsworth speak of 'poetry' they are not referring to the composition, the making of a poem, but to its mysterious and suprarational origin. They are saying, in effect, that you cannot consciously, through the exercise of will and intellect, force a poem into existence if the writer feels no compulsion to express, explore and shape a particular emotion or experience. But this does not mean that the actual writing of a poem is instinctive and unreflective: the spontaneous expression of emotion is a sigh, grunt, squeal or giggle; it is not a poem. The true poem is a work of art and a great deal of sheer labour, knowledge and skill must go into its making. Both Wordsworth and Keats, of course, were well aware of the truth of this, as even the most cursory glance at their manuscripts, with all the revisions, will show.

Prosody is a very complex science and countless volumes have been written on theories of versification. However, a great deal of the theorising is of only academic interest to specialists, and of little or no practical value to either the reader or writer of poetry. Therefore I propose to adopt a strictly utilitarian approach in this chapter and deal only with those aspects of verse technique, a knowledge of which I regard as indispensable to anyone who wishes to understand the basic mechanics of the subject.

The terminology of prosody derives from the Greek and, perhaps unfortunately, no indigenous English vocabulary has been coined to replace it; so in order to name the various devices of poetic technique we are forced to use words which might sound rather forbidding or exotic to ears unfamiliar with them. But the reader should not be intimidated by these words, and if he cannot remember them – if, for example, he cannot recall that the term for the metrical foot whose sound is ti-*tum*, as in the word 'today', is **iambic**, or the sound *tum*-ti, as in 'panic', is **trochaic** – it does not matter at all so long as his *ear* can recognise the difference in sound.

English is an **accentual** or **stress** language: this means that when we speak any word of more than one syllable, we pronounce one of the syllables with more weight or loudness than the other, or others. There are, of course, degrees of stress, but for the purpose of this simplified short study of prosody I shall put aside considerations of comparative weight of stress. Metre in English verse is based entirely on stress, and each line can be divided (or scanned) into its pattern of metrical feet. Here are four quotations from different poems which illustrate the four basic metrical feet employed by English poets. Other formal metres do exist, but they are so rarely employed that we need not trouble ourselves with naming them.

i   The curfew tolls the knell of parting day,
The lowing herd wind slowly o'er the lea,
The ploughman homeward plods his weary way,
And leaves the world to darkness and to me.

Thomas Gray (1716–1771)
Elegy Written in a Country Churchyard

ii   The Assyrian came down like the wolf on the fold,
And his cohorts were gleaming in purple and gold;
And the sheen of their spears was like stars on the sea,
When the blue wave rolls nightly on deep Galilee.

Lord Byron (1788–1824)
The Destruction of Sennacherib

iii   Willows whiten, aspens quiver,
Little breezes dusk and shiver
Thro' the wave that runs for ever
By the island in the river
        Flowing down to Camelot.

Alfred, Lord Tennyson (1809–1892)
The Lady of Shalott

iv   Take her up tenderly,
    Lift her with care;
Fashion'd so slenderly,
    Young and so fair.

Thomas Hood (1798–1845)
The Bridge of Sighs

iambic

The first quotation, from Gray's famous *Elegy*, is an impecc-
able demonstration of the iambic measure. Each line contains
five iambic feet and is called an **iambic pentameter**. The iambic metre is the most commonly used in English poetry: correct sonnets are all written in iambics; so is blank verse (not to
be confused with free verse, which obeys no metrical laws). If
we read Gray's lines slowly, aloud, exaggerating a little where
the stressed syllables fall, we find this pattern of sounds is
unmistakable (× = the unstressed syllable; \ = the stressed):

× \	× \	× \	× \	× \
The cur	few tolls	the knell	of part	ing day
1 (iambic foot)	2	3	4	5

Notice that the iambic movement is appropriate to the solemn,
measured tone of the *Elegy*.

anapaestic

The metre used by Byron in *The Destruction of Sennacherib* is
anapaestic, i.e. two unstressed syllables followed by one stressed (× × \).

× × \	× × \	× × \	× × \
The Assyr	ian came down	like the wolf	on the fold
1	2	3	4

Here the livelier, faster-moving metre suits the violent action
being described.

trochaic

The trochaic metre used by Tennyson in *The Lady of Shalott* is
the reverse of the iambic, the stress falling on the first of the
two-syllable foot: (\×)

\ ×	\ ×	\ ×	\ ×
Willows	whiten,	aspens	quiver
1	2	3	4

trochaic   Notice that the final unstressed syllable at the end of line 5 in
the quotation is dropped; this is done to avoid the risk of
monotony. The trochaic metre is light and tripping, but it is
not nearly as flexible as the iambic and may easily become
tedious if unrelieved by metrically contrasting lines.

dactylic

These lines from *The Bridge of Sighs* exemplify the use of dac-
tyls (reversed anapaests: $/\times\times$)

$$
\begin{array}{c|c}
\acute{}\quad\times\;\mid\;\times & \backslash\quad\times\;\times \\
\text{Take her up} & \text{tenderly} \\
1 & 2
\end{array}
$$

Here, again, the final unstressed syllable is dropped in the
second and fourth lines for the same purpose of avoiding
monotony.

Before going on briefly to discuss other aspects of prosody it
would seem a good idea to mention and quote from a remarkable poem which takes for its subject the art of poetry. The
Essay on Criticism was written by Alexander Pope (1688–
1744) when – almost incredibly – he was only twenty years of
age. The poem of some 744 lines is written in **heroic couplets**
– that is, in iambic pentameters which rhyme in pairs (and
occasionally in threes). In the following extract Pope not only
supplies a great deal of excellent practical criticism, but at the
same time actually demonstrates the principles he is expound-
ing. The word 'most' in the opening line refers to incompetent
critics.

> But most by *Numbers* judge a Poet's Song,
> And *smooth* or *rough*, with them, is *right* or *wrong*;
> In the bright *Muse* tho' thousand *Charms* conspire,
> Her *Voice* is all these tuneful Fools admire,
> 5 Who haunt *Parnassus* but to please their Ear,
> Not mend their Minds; as some to *Church* repair,
> Not for the *Doctrine*, but the *Musick* there.
> These *Equal Syllables* alone require,

Tho' oft the Ear the *open Vowels* tire,   dactylic
10   While *Expletives* their feeble Aid *do* join,
     And ten low Words oft creep in one dull Line,
     While they ring round the same *unvary'd Chimes*,
     With sure *Returns* of still *expected Rhymes*.
     Where-e'er you find *the cooling Western Breeze*,
15   In the next Line, it *whispers thro' the Trees*;
     If *Chrystal Streams with pleasing Murmurs creep*,
     The Reader's threaten'd (not in vain) with *Sleep*.
     Then, at the *last* and *only* Couplet fraught
     With some *unmeaning* Thing they call a *Thought*,
20   A *needless Alexandrine* ends the Song,
     That like a wounded Snake, drags its
                                 slow length along.
     Leave such to tune their own dull Rhimes, and know
     What's *roundly smooth*, or *languishingly slow*;
     And praise the *Easie Vigor* of a line,
25   Where *Denham's* Strength, and *Waller's*
                                 Sweetness join.
     True Ease in Writing comes from Art, not Chance,
     As those move easiest who have learn'd to dance.
     'Tis not enough no Harshness gives Offence,
     The *Sound* must seem an *Eccho* to the *Sense*.
30   *Soft* is the Strain when *Zephyr* gently blows,
     And the *smooth Stream* in *smoother Numbers* flows;
     But when loud Surges lash the sounding Shore,
     The *hoarse, rough Verse* shou'd like the *Torrent* roar.
     When *Ajax* strives, some Rocks' vast Weight to throw,
35   The Line too *labours*, and the Words move *slow*;
     Not so, when swift *Camilla* scours the plain,
     Flies o'er th'unbending Corn, and skims
                                 along the Main.

In the first eleven lines Pope attacks the view that metrical correctness is sufficient in itself to ensure total poetic effectiveness and, in lines 8 to 11, his own verse imitates the faults he is describing, perhaps most devastatingly in line 11 where, indeed, the ten flat monosyllables create just the effect he is censuring.

Next he condemns the use of obvious, cliché rhymes and again wittily illustrates this fault (lines 14 to 17) before attacking the practice of completing a poem or a stanza of a

dactylic

poem with an unnecessary Alexandrine (line 21). (An Alexandrine is a line of six iambic feet with a pause, or caesura, in the middle.)

In the last sixteen lines of the extract quoted Pope turns from attacking and illustrating faults to the constructive business of approving and demonstrating felicities of technique. Sir John Denham (1615–1659) was the author of a fine topographical poem, *Cooper's Hill*, and Sir Edmund Waller (1606–1687) wrote the beautiful lyric, *Go, Lovely Rose*. Pope states that mere smoothness of metre is not enough, but the sound of the words should imitate or echo the action being described (lines 28 and 29), and in the following two lines he shows the reader just how this should be done with the cunningly placed repetitions of 's'-sounds and the murmurous 'm'-sounds and the slow, open vowels in 'smooth', 'Stream', 'Numbers', and 'flows'. Similarly the succeeding lines demonstrate splendidly how a skilful manipulation of rhythm and appropriate vowel and consonant sounds can 'seem an echo to the Sense'.

alliteration

This is the term given to the deliberate repetition of the same consonant sound, but it is important to understand that such a repetition employed for its own sake, and not in order to imitate the sound of the thing being described, is of no value. The alliterative 's's and 'm's referred to above (line 31) sigh and murmur like the breeze itself.

assonance

In lines 36 and 37 the smoothly skimming sense is achieved partly by the alliteration of 's' and the hard 'c' (or 'k') sound, and is also greatly assisted by another echoing, that of the same repeated *vowel* sound. This is known as assonance. The repetition here is of the short 'i'-sound in 'swift', 'Camilla', and 'skims'. Assonance is also effectively employed in lines 34 and 35. Here the open 'a'-sounds are repeated in 'Ajax', 'weight'

and 'labours', slowing down the movement of the lines and
increasing the sense of effort, of heaving.

rhyme

Pope's *Essay on Criticism* rhymes throughout, though of
course not all verse need make use of the device (see **blank
verse** on page 00). However, rhyme is used in almost all lyrical
and in many narrative forms such as the Ballad. Quite simply
full rhyme – or ordinary rhyme – consists of two words or final
syllables of words which sound exactly alike except for the
initial consonant sound – e.g. bleat/meet, trite/sight, peace/
lease, etc. In polysyllabic rhymes only the final syllable, or syllables, need correspond – e.g. elation/sensation, intersection/
affection.

Rhymes are masculine or feminine. Rhymes which
occur on stressed syllables are **masculine. Feminine** rhymes
are those of two or more syllables in which the stressed and
rhyming syllables are not the final ones – e.g. diverging/surg-
ing, abruptly/corruptly. Women's Lib supporters might
reasonably object to the weak, unstressed syllables being
designated 'feminine', but the vocabulary of prosody is, I am
afraid, intransigently old-fashioned.

All monosyllabic rhymes, of course, must be masculine. Rhyming words of two or more syllables are masculine if
the final syllable is stressed – e.g. desire/conspire, concen-
trate/felicitate.

End rhyme or **terminal rhyme** is the most common
type, and is exemplified in Pope's rhymed couplets (my italics):

> True Ease in Writing comes from Art, not *Chance,*
> As those move easiest who have learn'd to *dance.*

Internal rhyme occurs when the rhymes appear within the
body of the line or lines, obviously as in (my italics):

> See the *size* of her *thighs,* the part of her lips. . .
>
> John Betjeman

rhyme But perhaps less obviously as in Dylan Thomas's lines from *Fern Hill* (my italics):

> My wishes raced *through* the house HIGH hay
> And nothing I cared, at my SKY-*blue* trades, that
> time allows
> In all his tuneful turning such *few* and such
> morning songs. . .

Near rhyme – sometimes called **slant rhyme** or **off rhyme** – is less easy to define because its recognition depends on the ear of the person reading the poem. It occurs when two words are very similar in sound and shape, as in 'turning' and 'morning', used in the last line quoted above, but they are not full rhymes since the vowel sounds are different. A full rhyme for 'turning' would be 'churning' or 'burning', and for 'morning', 'adorning'.

There is a particular kind of near rhyme which can be described with precision. This is called **consonantal rhyme** or **pararhyme** and was used a great deal by Wilfred Owen in his poetry of the First World War. In pararhyme the consonant sounds of the two related words are identical, but the vowel sound must differ: e.g. *lap/lip, drift/draught, mystery/mastery*. The dissonance or slightly harsh, off-key effect of pararhyme seemed especially suitable for the brutal subject matter of much of Owen's poetry. Here is the opening stanza of *Exposure*, where pararhyme is used at the end of the first four lines, rhyming **ABBA.**

> Our brains ache, in the merciless iced east winds
> that knife us. . . **A**
> Wearied we keep awake because the night
> is silent. . . **B**
> Low, drooping flares confuse our memory of the
> salient. . . **B**
> Worried by silence, sentries whisper,
> curious, nervous, **A**
> But nothing happens.

rhyming forms

I cannot conclude this chapter on the poet's craft without a mention of some of the traditional poetic forms which are available to the English poet for either his imitation or adaptation. **Heroic couplets**, which we have seen so ably handled by Pope in the extract from *Essay on Criticism,* may be of two kinds: **closed couplets** and **open couplets.** Pope employs the closed couplet, that is, two iambic pentameters using end rhyme, forming a complete unit of sense:

> 'Tis not enough no Harshness gives Offence,
> The *Sound* must seem an *Eccho* to the *Sense.*

The closed couplet, as you will see above, is self-contained; it makes a complete statement. The open couplet differs in that the sense runs on into the next couplet, as here in a short extract from Byron's *English Bards and Scotch Reviewers:*

> Who in soft guise, surrounded by a choir
> Of virgins melting, not to Vesta's fire,
> With sparkling eyes, and cheek by passion flushed
> Strikes his wild lyre, while listening dames are
> hushed?

Rhymed couplets may be used in other metres than iambic pentameter, and the most common alternative is rhymed tetrameter (a line of four iambic feet). A good example of rhymed tetrameter is the beautiful and witty *To His Coy Mistress* by Andrew Marvell (1621–1678), which begins:

> Had we but world enough, and time,
> This coyness, lady, were no crime.
> We would sit down, and think which way
> To walk, and pass our long love's day.
> Thou by the Indian Ganges' side
> Should'st rubies find: I by the tide
> Of Humber would complain. I would
> Love you ten years before the Flood,
> And you should, if you please, refuse
> Till the conversion of the Jews.

rhyming forms

A great favourite among English verse forms is the **quatrain,** a stanza, in any metre, of four lines. The **ballad stanza** is a quatrain of alternate tetrameters and trimeters, usually rhyming **ABCB,** as in:

The king sits in Dunfermline towne	**A**
Drinking the blood-red wine;	**B**
'O where will I get a skilful skipper	**C**
To sail this ship of mine?'	**B**

The stanza form used in Gray's *Elegy Written in a Country Churchyard* is known as the **heroic quatrain** and it consists of four iambic pentameters, rhyming **ABAB:**

The curfew tolls the knell of parting day,	**A**
The lowing herd wind slowly o'er the lea,	**B**
The ploughman homeward plods his weary way,	**A**
And leaves the world to darkness and to me.	**B**

Tennyson, in his great poem to the memory of his friend Arthur Henry Hallam who died tragically young, uses a quatrain which has come to be known as the **In Memoriam stanza,** from the title of the poem, *In Memoriam.* The four lines are iambic tetrameters, rhyming **ABBA:**

Be near me when the sensuous frame	**A**
Is rack'd with pangs that conquer trust;	**B**
And Time, a maniac scattering dust,	**B**
And Life, a Fury slinging flame.	**A**

Six-line stanzas are quite commonly used and one, known as the **stave of six,** can be in either pentameter or tetrameter, rhyming ABABCC. Matthew Arnold (1822–1888) showed a fondness for the tetrameter form of the stave of six:

But when the moon their hollows lights,	**A**
And they are swept by balms of spring,	**B**
And in their glens, on starry nights,	**A**
The nightingales divinely sing;	**B**
And lovely notes, from shore to shore,	**C**
Across the sounds and channels pour –	**C**

To Marguerite

Rhyme royal or the **Chaucerian stanza** (used in Chaucer's

Troilus and Criseyde) consists of seven pentameters, rhyming **ABABBCC,** though the final line, as in the stanza quoted below from Wordsworth's *Resolution and Independence,* may be a hexameter (a line of six feet):

All things that love the sun are out of doors;	A
The sky rejoices in the morning's birth;	B
The grass is bright with rain-drops; – on the moors	A
The hare is running races in her mirth;	B
And with her feet she from the plashy earth	B
Raises a mist, that, glittering in the sun,	C
Runs with her all the way, wherever she doth run.	C

Ottava rima is probably the most common of the English eight-line stanzas, and it is the form employed by Lord Byron in his comic masterpiece, *Don Juan,* an extract from which is given below. All eight lines are pentameters and they rhyme **ABABABCC:**

He turned his lip to hers, and with his hand	A
Called back the tangles of her wandering hair;	B
Even then their love they could not all command,	A
And half forgot their danger and despair:	B
Antonia's patience now was at a stand –	A
'Come, come, 'tis no time now for fooling there,'	B
She whispered, in great wrath – 'I must deposit	C
This pretty gentleman within the closet.'	C

Edmund Spenser (1552–1599) invented a special stanza for his immensely long allegory, *The Faerie Queene.* The **Spenserian stanza** consists of nine lines rhyming ABABBCBCC, the first eight being pentameters and the ninth a hexameter. A couple of centuries after Spenser, John Keats (1795–1821) made splendid use of the form in *The Eve of St Agnes:*

And still she slept an azure-lidded sleep,	A
In blanchèd linen, smooth, and lavendered,	B
While he from forth the closet brought a heap	A
Of candied apple, quince, and plum, and gourd;	B
With jellies soother than the creamy curd,	B
And lucent syrops, tinct with cinnamon;	C
Manna and dates, in argosy transferred	B
From Fez; and spicèd dainties, every one	C
From silken Samarcand to cedared Lebanon.	C

There are various other regular stanza forms but they are used so infrequently that they are of interest only to specialists in prosody. The **ode,** for example, though in its original form a most elaborate formal structure, has come in English to apply to almost any poem of some length, the form of which does not fit into any other category. Most English odes still possess some kind of metrical complexity and are usually concerned with celebrating or commemorating their subject, whether it be a person (Marvell's *Ode on Cromwell's Return from Ireland*), the weather (Shelley's *Ode to the West Wind*), an object (Keats's *Ode on a Grecian Urn*), and so on. However, we cannot leave the subject of prescribed poetic forms without mention of the sonnet, blank verse and free verse.

The **sonnet** is the most widely used single-stanza form in English poetry. It consists of fourteen lines, each one an iambic pentameter, and there are two distinct kinds of sonnet, the **Italian or Petrarchan** and the **English or Shakespearian.** The Italian sonnet is divided into two parts, the first eight lines forming the octave and the last six the sestet. The rhyme scheme of the octave is always **ABBAABBA,** while that of the sestet may vary but is usually either **CDECDE** or **CDCDCD.** The division of octave and sestet should be used by the poet to show some kind of development, or shift of thought or feeling, introduced by the sestet. Here is a famous Italian sonnet by John Keats, *On First Looking into Chapman's Homer:*

Much have I travelled in the realms of gold,	A
And many goodly states and kingdoms seen;	B
Round many western islands have I been	B
Which bards in fealty to Apollo hold.	A
Oft of one wide expanse had I been told,	A
That deep-browed Homer ruled as his demesne:	B
Yet did I never breathe its pure serene	B
Till I heard Chapman speak out loud and bold:	A
Then felt I like some watcher of the skies	C
When a new planet swims into his ken;	D
Or like stout Cortez when with eagle eyes	C
He stared at the Pacific – and all his men	D
Looked at each other with a wild surmise –	C
Silent, upon a peak in Darien.	D

In the octave Keats, using the metaphor of travel and explora-

tion, speaks of his restricted spiritual and intellectual jour-
neyings (that is, his reading of the minor poets) but the mighty
work of Homer was something he knew only by repute until
he read Chapman's (an Elizabethan poet) fine translation into
English of the Greek poet's complete works. Then, at the
beginning of the sestet, the metaphor changes from travelling
to astronomy: the theme of exploration and discovery is
developed but in different terms, and it concludes with a
return to the original idea, now given a solid and dramatic
sense of reality by the introduction of a particular historic
figure, Cortez (Keats in fact was mistaken – it was Balboa who
was the first European to gaze on the Pacific) and a particular
place.

The English or Shakespearian sonnet is not divided
into octave and sestet, and it always ends with a rhymed couplet. So, just as there must be a relationship of tension, agree-
ment, contradiction or elaboration between octave and sestet
in the Italian sonnet, there must be a similar relationship
between the final couplet and the preceding twelve lines (or
three quatrains) in the English sonnet.

The rhyme scheme of the English sonnet is **ABABC-
DCDEFEFGG,** and here is an example from Shakespeare himself:

That time of year thou may'st in me behold	**A**
When yellow leaves, or none, or few, do hang	**B**
Upon those boughs which shake against the cold –	**A**
Bare ruined choirs, where late the sweet birds sang.	**B**
In me thou seest the twilight of such day	**C**
As after sunset fadeth in the west,	**D**
Which by-and-by black night doth take away,	**C**
Death's second self, that seals up all in rest:	**D**
In me thou seest the glowing of such fire	**E**
That on the ashes of his youth doth lie,	**F**
As the death-bed whereon it must expire,	**E**
Consumed with that which it was nourished by.	**F**
This thou perceiv'st, which makes thy love more strong	**G**
To love that well which thou must leave ere long.	**G**

Notice that the first twelve lines consist of three complete sense units or statements, each of four lines, and these could reasonably be printed as separate quatrains. However, all three statements deal with a single subject, that of mortality, the approach of old age and death; the metaphors (or images) used are of an autumn tree, a sunset, and a dying fire. The final couplet makes its comment quite plainly, without metaphor, on the significance of the images used. He says, in effect, to the person to whom the poem is addressed: 'You can see that I am nearing the end of my life, but the effect of this is to strengthen the intensity of your love because you know that its object will soon be removed.' The couplet affirms the living strength of human love and counterpoints it against the images of decay that have gone before.

blank verse

Finally, a few notes on blank verse and free verse: **blank verse** consists quite simply of lines of iambic pentameter which possess no end rhymes. In one sense it is the easiest form in which to write verse, but, since the only rule the poet has to obey is that his lines should each contain five iambic feet, it is a lot less easy for him to avoid a dull, mechanical monotony. The great writers of blank verse, such as Marlowe, Shakespeare, Milton, Wordsworth and Browning, avoid this monotony by various devices which are best shown by example. Here is part of a famous speech from Shakespeare's last play, *The Tempest*:

> Our revels now are ended. These our actors,
> As I foretold you, were all spirits, and
> Are melted into air, into thin air;
> And, like the baseless fabric of this vision,
> The cloud-capped towers, the gorgeous palaces,
> The solemn temples, the great globe itself,
> Yea, all which it inherit, shall dissolve,
> And, like this insubstantial pageant faded,
> Leave not a rack behind.

Notice how, apart from the marvellous resonances of the lan-   **blank verse**
guage, Shakespeare sustains an easy, conversational flow by
varying the placing of the stresses (the feet are not always
strictly iambic) and using feminine endings (unstressed syllables) at the conclusion of some lines.

Blank verse is not used only by poets of the past. Wallace Stevens, a twentieth-century American poet, is a superb
exponent of the metre. Here are just a few lines from his
poem, *Sunday Morning:*

> Deer walk upon our mountains, and the quail
> Whistle about us their spontaneous cries;
> Sweet berries ripen in the wilderness;
> And, in the isolation of the sky,
> At evening, casual flocks of pigeons make
> Ambiguous undulations as they sink,
> Downward to darkness, on extended wings.

The iambic metre is almost completely regular (line 2 and the
final line begin with a stressed syllable), but the rhythmical
variety is achieved by subtly juxtaposing polysyllabic words
with monosyllables, and the sound is indeed 'an *Eccho* to the
Sense'. Observe how, in the last two lines, the rising pitch and
rhythm of 'undulations' falls with 'as they sink,/Downwards to
darkness, on extended wings'. And the stretched syllables of
'extended wings' mime the outspreading of the birds' wings.

free verse

This is sometimes confused with blank verse because both
dispense with rhyme. In fact free verse is almost impossible to
define except in negative terms: it is verse because it is written in lines, but it does not conform to any metrical principles.
Some free verse seems to derive from the sonorous rhythms of
the Authorised Version of the Old Testament. Christopher
Smart (1722–1771) wrote an extraordinary religious poem called *Jubilate Agno* which clearly owes its rhythmic movement
to the Bible, but free verse as we understand it is a fairly modern prosodic development and its generally acknowledged
father is the American Walt Whitman (1819–1892). Here is an
example of Whitman's free verse:

free verse

> In the dooryard fronting an old farm-house near the
> white-wash'd palings,
> Stands the lilac-bush tall-growing with heart-shaped
> leaves of rich green,
> With many a pointed blossom rising delicate, with the
> perfume strong I love,
> With every leaf a miracle — and from this bush in the
> dooryard,
> With delicate-color'd blossoms and heart-shaped
> leaves of rich green,
> A sprig with its flower I break.

While there is obviously no metrical regularity in these lines they do seem to conform to a rough, instinctive aural pattern, and certainly the device of repetition of both phrasing and isolated words must be intentional. It could claim to be verse because it is too insistently rhythmical, too conscious of itself, to be plain prose.

More influential than Whitman on contemporary writers of free verse, of which there are many (some would say too many), were the experiments of D. H. Lawrence and the Americans Ezra Pound and William Carlos Williams. Lawrence, after writing many poems in conventional metre, decided that the regularity of traditional verse was too restrictive and he came to believe, in theory and in practice, that poetic rhythm was more '. . . a matter of movements in space than footsteps hitting the earth . . . it doesn't depend on the ear, particularly, but on the sensitive soul . . .'. Ezra Pound and W. C. Williams believed that the old metrical cadences were no longer appropriate to the tempo of living in the twentieth century, and that a new prosody had to be constructed, but I see little evidence that their examples have enriched the poetic possibilities of our times. The fact is that, while pleasing poems have been written in free verse, a great deal of what, in this form, passes for poetry is in fact prose — and often miserably inferior prose — arranged on the page to resemble the shape of verse. I respect any poet's wish to find new modes of expression and extend the boundaries of his art, but I believe that he is more likely to find a path to these ends through a study of traditional prosody than in depending on 'the sensitive soul'.

4

NARRATIVE POETRY

It is almost certainly true that the earliest origins of the art of poetry lie in the magical rites of primitive man, and its strong rhythmical nature is clearly related to the rhythms of dance. It is reasonable to suppose that when our remote pagan ancestors attempted to influence the powers of the gods or of nature by dance and mime, their physical movements were accompanied by words which were chanted in time to the ordered pattern of their steps. The earliest poetry was incantatory and the element of magic, of the mysterious, of the inexplicable, has always been a necessary presence in authentic poems. But, as the arts evolved and became separate from their primitive ritualistic origins, and became in fact autonomous, giving pleasure for purely aesthetic, non-utilitarian reasons, verbal art moved from pure incantation to mimesis, that is the imitation of external reality and behaviour, and towards the imposition of pattern, not merely the pattern of language but of the events embodied by the words. In short, the art of story-telling or narrative was born.

Among the earliest narrative poems in English are the anonymous ballads which belong to the oral tradition: these story-poems, composed in short stanzas, almost invariably quatrains using strong regular metre and rhyme, were passed from generation to generation by word of mouth, so it is impossible to attribute precise dates of composition. It is generally accepted by literary historians that most originate from the fifteenth century, although there must have been many in existence before that period because Chaucer, in the latter part of the fourteenth century, produced parodies of the form in the *Canterbury Tales.*

ballad

The word 'ballad' derives from the late Latin *ballare* meaning 'to dance' ('ballet' has the same source), and the earliest ballads were intended to accompany music and dance. We retain that original meaning when we speak, for instance, of the sentimental ballads or popular songs so much enjoyed by our Victorian ancestors. The narrative ballads, too, were in their original form almost certainly sung and supported by some kind of musical accompaniment, and that 'singable' quality has remained a feature of the ballad until the present day, though some of the modern practitioners of the old ballad form, such as W. H. Auden and Charles Causley, have introduced a sophistication of imagery and thought that would be alien to the more primitive verse-tales. Not that the early ballads are without deeper levels of meaning than their simple stories might lead the casual reader to suppose. They deal mostly with fairly violent events and frequently with the themes of betrayal, loss and revenge. What gives them their enduring quality, however, is not the moral or allegorical message that they might contain, but the fact that the images used are generally ones of permanent and haunting power and, despite the extreme simplicity of the form, quite subtle effects are often achieved. Here is the whole of *Sir Patrick Spens:*

> The king sits in Dunfermline towne
> Drinking the blood-red wine;
> 'O where will I get a skilful skipper
> To sail this ship of mine?'

Up and spake an elder knight, **ballad**
    Sat at the king's right knee:
'Sir Patrick Spens is the best sailor
    That ever sailed the sea.'

The king has written a broad letter
    And sealed it with his hand,
And sent it to Sir Patrick Spens
    Was walking on the strand.

'To Noroway, to Noroway,
    To Noroway o'er the foam;
The King's own daughter of Noroway,
    'Tis thou must bring her home!'

The first line that Sir Patrick read
    A loud, loud laugh laughed he:
The next line that Sir Patrick read
    The tear blinded his ee.

'Oh who is this has done this deed,
    This ill deed unto me;
To send me out this time o' the year
    To sail upon the sea?

'Make haste, make haste, my merry men all,
    Our good ship sails the morn.'
'Oh say not so, my master dear,
    For I fear a deadly storm.

'I saw the new moon late yestere'en
    With the old moon in her arm;
And if we go to sea, master,
    I fear we'll come to harm.'

They had not sailed a league, a league,
    A league, but barely three,
When the sky grew dark, the wind blew loud,
    And angry grew the sea.

The anchor broke, the topmast split,
    'Twas such a deadly storm.
The waves came over the broken ship
    Till all her sides were torn.

O long, long may the ladies sit
    With their fans into their hand,
Or ere they see Sir Patrick Spens
    Come sailing to the strand.

ballad

O long, long may the maidens stand
    With their gold combs in their hair,
Before they'll see their own dear loves
    Come home to greet them there.

O forty miles off Aberdeen
    'Tis fifty fathom deep.
And there lies good Sir Patrick Spens
    With the Scots lords at his feet.

This poem possesses an obvious appeal: the pounding rhythms are invigorating, the tragic story simple. But its anonymous author employs devices which show that he was a shrewd craftsman. That opening quatrain sets the narrative into swift motion with the utmost economy and the description of the wine as 'blood-red' insinuates from the start a hint of menace. The repetitions: 'Noroway to Noroway . . .', 'Make haste, make haste . . .', 'A league, a league . . .', 'O long, long may . . .' are strongly mnemonic and the description of the storm is a model of evocative understatement.

    In the following modern ballad by a living poet, Charles Causley, there is a slightly greater sophistication of both form and content, but the family resemblance to its ancient precursors is unmistakable. Where *Sir Patrick Spens* is written in quatrains of tetrameters and trimeters rhyming **abcb,** *The Faithless Wife* uses trimeters, except for the third line in each stanza which is a tetrameter containing an additional internal rhyme. The allegorical content is explicitly underlined at the end of the poem where, perhaps unnecessarily, the poet explains that the faithless wife is a personification of Peace, and the soldier of War.

Ballad of the Faithless Wife

Carry her down to the river
    Carry her down to the sea
Let the bully-boys stare at her braided hair
    But never a glance from me.

Down by the writhing water
    Down by the innocent sand
They laid my bride by the toiling tide
    A stone in her rifled hand.

Under the dainty eagle   **ballad**
   Under the ravening dove
Under a high and healthy sky
   I waited for my love.

Off she ran with a soldier
   Tall as a summer tree,
Soft as a mouse he came to my house
   And stole my love from me.

O splintered were all the windows
   And broken all the chairs
War like a knife ran through my life
   And the blood ran down the stairs.

Loud on the singing morning
   I hear the mad birds rise
Safe from harm to the sun's alarm
   As the sound of fighting dies.

I would hang my harp on the branches
   And weep all through the day
But stranger, see! The wounded tree
   Has burned itself away.

False O false was my lover
   Dead on the diamond shore
White as a fleece, for her name was Peace
   And the soldier's name was War.

allegory

The term 'allegory' derives from the Latin and means, literally,
the use of language to say something other than what the words
seem to be saying. The parables of Christ are allegories.
Edmund Spenser's *The Faerie Queen* is an allegory, or sequence
of allegories, in which various abstract virtues such as courtesy,
chastity, friendship, justice and religious truth are personified
and celebrated in stories of knightly adventure. *The Faerie
Queen* is unquestionably an important landmark in English
literature but, because so many of the references are
unintelligible to all except the specialist, and because the
regularity of the Spenserian stanza becomes so soporifically
monotonous, it is probably best left to those specialists, though

allegory   some of the descriptive passages, such as the account of the
Cave of Mammon in Book II, can give considerable enjoyment to
the general reader.

Chaucer's *Canterbury Tales,* though written two hundred years earlier, in the late fourteenth century, is still
eminently readable once the minor difficulty of mastering the
unfamiliar syntax and vocabulary of Middle English has been
surmounted. There are plenty of 'translations' of the *Tales* into
modern English but even the best of these, such as the one by
Neville Coghill, lose a great deal of the sparkle and energy of
the original language.

The tales are recounted by the various pilgrims who
gather at the Tabard Inn in Southwark for the purpose of
travelling to pay homage at the shrine of Becket in Canterbury. There are twenty-three tales – though Chaucer originally planned that each of the thirty-one pilgrims would tell
four stories each – and they are wonderfully varied in content
and mood, covering the romantic and chivalric, the moral allegorical, and the plain comic and bawdy.

epic

The *Canterbury Tales,* as the title suggests, is a heterogeneous
collection of anecdotes, not a sustained narrative. The epic
form, however, is always a continuous narrative and, traditionally, it is one which celebrates the heroic achievements of
some great figure from history or mythology; the great epics of
classical literature are the Greek *Iliad* and *Odyssey* (attri-
buted to Homer) and the Latin *Aeneid* of Virgil. The only true
epic poem in the English language is Milton's *Paradise Lost,*
first printed in 1667, and this massive work, composed in
blank verse, takes for its subject nothing less than the Fall of
Man. The poem is divided into twelve books (it was originally
conceived by Milton as ten) and the wealth of biblical allusion
may present problems for many modern readers. Nevertheless the symphonic splendour of the language may be readily
enjoyed, and at least some familiarity with the work is not
merely desirable but quite necessary to any serious student of
the development of English blank verse.

satire

A narrative genre in which English poetry has excelled, especially in the seventeenth and eighteenth centuries, is that of satire. Literary satire may be defined as a verbal attack upon corruption, folly or vice, whether manifested in persons or in institutions, using the weapon of ridicule. John Dryden's *Absalom and Achitophel,* published in 1681, was very popular in its own time and, despite its being, by its nature , aimed at a particular audience in a particular time and place, it can still give much pleasure and entertainment through its wit and brilliant handling of the heroic couplet. It deals with the attempt by Lord Shaftesbury's party to exclude the Duke of York from the succession to Charles II's throne and to replace him by the Duke of Monmouth. The various characters involved are given biblical names: Monmouth becomes Absalom, the son of King David who rebelled against his father; Shaftesbury is Achitophel who, in the Old Testament, conspired with Absalom against King David; Charles II is David and the Duke of Buckingham is Zimri, the servant and murderer of the King of Judah, and so on. Here are just a few lines from *Absalom and Achitophel,* describing Buckingham, but even in this brief extract the reader may taste the astringent flavour of Dryden's sardonic wit:

> In the first rank of these did Zimri stand:
> A man so various that he seemed to be
> Not one, but all mankind's epitome.
> Stiff in opinions, always in the wrong,
> Was everything by starts and nothing long;
> But in the course of one revolving moon
> Was chemist, fiddler, statesman, and buffoon.

The two great satirical poets of the eighteenth century whose work can be read today with enjoyment are Alexander Pope, '1688–1744 *(The Rape of the Lock, The Dunciad* and, most strongly recommended, *Epistle to Doctor Arbuthnot)* and Jonathan Swift, 1667–1745 *(Verses on the Death of Doctor Swift).* Swift, who was a cousin of Dryden, is best known for his prose satire *Gulliver's Travels,* though his verse shows remarkable qualities of energy, wit and intelligence. But what to my mind is unquestionably the most entertaining and generally delightful satirical poem in the English language is *Don Juan* by Lord Byron, published in sections between 1819 and 1824 and comprising sixteen cantos written in ottava rima. This very long poem, which was never finished, uses the life and adventures of the fictitious Don Juan, a young gentleman of Seville, who after a love affair at the age of sixteen with the delectable Donna Julia is sent abroad by his mother. He is shipwrecked and cast away on a Greek island where he meets Haidée, the lovely daughter of a pirate who is believed to be dead but returns to the island to exact vengeance on the young man by selling him into slavery. Many more improbable adventures and love affairs follow, but the story is principally a richly entertaining scaffold which supports the poet's shrewd, funny and often vitriolic comments on contemporary life and letters in England.

The most remarkable thing about *Don Juan* is that the poem supplies inexhaustible pleasure to the twentieth-century reader without demanding any specialised knowledge of the literature or historical background of Byron's times, and the verse form employed, although unvarying in metrical regularity, never becomes remotely tedious. The author contrives to sustain an easy colloquial flow and he modulates comfortably from the mock heroic and lyrical modes to the broadest slapstick, while the sheer narrative pace sweeps the reader effortlessly and delightedly along. Here, from Canto I (stanzas 106 to 109), is the beginning of Juan's first intimate encounter with the lovely Donna Julia:

> How beautiful she looked! Her conscious heart
>   Glowed in her cheek, and yet she felt no wrong,
> Oh Love, how perfect is thy mystic art,
>   Strengthening the weak and trampling on the strong.
> How self-deceitful is the sagest part
>   Of mortals whom thy lure hath led along.
> The precipice she stood on was immense,
> So was her creed in her own innocence.

> She thought of her own strength and Juan's youth
>   And of the folly of all prudish fears,
> Victorious virtue and domestic truth,
>   And then of Don Alfonso's fifty years.

I wish these last had not occurred in sooth,   **satire**
    Because that number rarely much endears
And through all climes, the snowy and the sunny,
Sounds ill in love, whate'er it may in money.

When people say, 'I've told you fifty times,'
    They mean to scold and very often do.
When poets say, 'I've written fifty rhymes,'
    They make you dread that they'll recite them too.
In gangs of fifty, thieves commit their crimes.
    At fifty love for love is rare, 'tis true;
But then no doubt it equally as true is,
A good deal may be bought for fifty louis.

By the time Queen Victoria had ascended the throne in 1837 the English novel had become not only a popular literary form, but a respectable one. It is important to remember, when surveying the development of literature in England, that virtually all imaginative writing, narrative and descriptive, was until the eighteenth century in verse, and the prose narrative, principally in the form of the novel, did not begin to take over territory formerly commanded by the poet until the mid-nineteenth century. In other words, until then the long narrative poem was as likely, or – among the educated middle classes – *more* likely, to be read than the novel. The last story-poems of considerable length to be written by accomplished poets were the quite elaborately plotted works of Browning (*The Ring and the Book*), Tennyson (*Maud*), and Arnold (*Sohrab and Rustum*). Since then poets have, almost without exception, left the long story to the novelists, tacitly acknowledging that prose, with its free rhythms and relative lack of formal restraints, is much more suitable for the recounting of a tale of substantial length and complexity. This does not mean, however, that the narrative element disappeared at that point from English poetry.

    The take-over of so much of what was formerly the poet's undisputed territory – including biography and political satire as well as fiction – by writers of prose resulted in post-Victorian poetry becoming more compressed. A kind of narrative poem emerged which might be described as the short narrative lyric. The ancestry of this form can be traced back to the early ballads, but it tends to become much shorter and does not confine itself to one set metrical and rhyming pattern. Many of the short poems of Thomas Hardy fall into this category: they are brief tales, each of which has its appropriate metre and verse form. Here is one example:

Outside the Window

'My stick!' he says, and turns in the lane
To the house just left, whence a vixen voice
Comes out with the firelight through the pane,
And he sees within that the girl of his choice
Stands rating her mother with eyes aglare
For something said while he was there.

'At last I behold her soul undraped!'
Thinks the man who had loved her more than himself;
'My God! – 'tis but narrowly I have escaped. –
My precious porcelain proves it delf.'
His face has reddened like one ashamed,
And he steals off, leaving his stick unclaimed.

Now this mordant little anecdote could just as easily have been told in prose, as a short story, but in that form it would lose much of its impact. Hardy wastes no time in setting the scene. He does not describe the appearance of the three characters or comment on their age, temperament and antecedents: he focuses on the dramatic core and cuts away all that is inessential, leaving the reader to supply such material from his own imagination if he so wishes. What is unsaid is almost as important as what is stated, for the poem works upon the reader's imagination after the text has been put aside. We know that the man, the girl's suitor, did not return, and we cannot help wondering what drama ensued between mother and daughter when the girl realised that she had been abandoned.

The device of paring down, of producing a quintessence of a story, has been developed and refined by many poets in the present century to the point where almost all conventional narrative is omitted and a single image or pattern of images presented. Poems of this kind are like icebergs. The reader can examine only the tip, but from this he may deduce

the major, hidden part. W. H. Auden had written a tiny poem
of only eight lines called *Gare du Midi:*

> A nondescript express in from the South,
> Crowds round the ticket barrier, a face
> To welcome which the mayor has not contrived
> Bugles or braid: something about the mouth
> Distracts the stray look with alarm and pity.
> Snow is falling. Clutching a little case,
> He walks out briskly to infect a city
> Whose terrible future may have just arrived.

This poem was written in the 1930s at a time of grave international unrest, when the menacing shade of Fascism darkened
the lives of all Europeans. It was also a time of tortuous political intrigue and double-dealing, of espionage and counter-
espionage, when every capital city was infested by agents,
schemers, hired political assassins and the like. Certain novelists were fascinated by the dramatic possibilities of the scene,
among them Graham Greene who wrote an excellent thriller,
A Gun for Sale, about a hired killer who is employed to assas-
sinate a foreign Head of State, with the object of triggering off
a world war. The book is charged with an atmosphere of danger, corruption and impending disaster, both personal and
international, and Auden's poem captures a strikingly similar
note of menace, suggesting, too, the desperate loneliness of
the assassin, his ability to arouse both fear and pity, his absurd
inadequacy as a human being which is terrifyingly allied to
his power to destroy.

Philip Larkin, one of our finest living poets, is adept in
the use of the partially submerged narrative. Here is one such,
entitled *Mr Bleaney:*

> 'This was Mr Bleaney's room. He stayed
> The whole time he was at the Bodies, till
> They moved him.' Flowered curtains, thin and frayed,
> Fall to within five inches of the sill,
>
> Whose window shows a strip of building land,
> Tussocky, littered. 'Mr Bleaney took
> My bit of garden properly in hand.'
> Bed, upright chair, sixty-watt bulb, no hook

Behind the door, no room for books or bags –
'I'll take it.' So it happens that I lie
Where Mr Bleaney lay, and stub my fags
On the same saucer-souvenir, and try

Stuffing my ears with cotton-wool, to drown
The jabbering set he egged her on to buy.
I know his habits – what time he came down,
His preference for sauce to gravy, why

He kept on plugging at the four aways –
Likewise their yearly frame: the Frinton folk
Who put him up for summer holidays,
And Christmas at his sister's house in Stoke.

But if he stood and watched the frigid wind
Tousling the clouds, lay on the fusty bed
Telling himself that this was home, and grinned,
And shivered, without shaking off the dread

That how we live measures our own nature,
And at his age having no more to show
Than one hired box should make him pretty sure
He warranted no better, I don't know.

Here the poet makes use of many of the techniques of the writer of prose fiction, including dialogue, description of place and naming of characters, but he eliminates all that might weaken the sense of desolation that he wishes to convey. The poem opens with the words spoken by the landlady who is showing a vacant bed-sitter to the narrator. She refers to the previous tenant, a Mr Bleaney, who worked for a firm with the rather ominous name of the Bodies before he was transferred, presumably to another branch of the same company. The view from the window, and the room itself, are bleak and unwelcoming, but the narrator, who clearly is in no position to be selective, agrees to rent it. After the words, 'I'll take it', in the second line of the third quatrain, there is an implied cut or time-switch to a future in which the narrator has learned from his landlady's gossip and from the conditions that he has inherited a good deal about his predecessor, his habits, distractions, where he spent his dismal holidays, and so on. Then, in the last two stanzas, the poem moves into the region of what the narrator does *not* know about Mr Bleaney but can only surmise: did the former tenant share the same thoughts and feelings as his successor, the terror that 'how we live measures our own nature', that, to put it crudely, we get what we deserve?

Mr Bleaney is a harsh, unconsoling look at a certain kind of reality. Some readers and critics have been deterred by what they regard as its pessimism and negative surrender to inimical circumstance, but I feel that this is a shallow response to the poem's multi-layered content, and it misses the point that *Mr Bleaney* is a fiction. Larkin has employed the iceberg narrative to tell us quite a lot about the way in which multitudes of people spend their lives: the day-to-day routine seems unbearably tedious, yet it is endured by so many and perhaps even enjoyed. What in some people's lives may seem to others intolerable, may not be so – almost always *is* not so to the participants. Larkin's narrator appears to be disconsolate: his view of his own condition would seem to approach that of total despair, but the curious and comforting paradox is that the poet has created an intricate, truthful and darkly witty work of art from such unlikely material and his success in doing so is a kind of affirmation of life itself.

In this chapter I have attempted only to provide a simplified and necessarily limited survey of narrative poetry in the English language. Many great and renowned narrative poems such as Coleridge's *The Ancient Mariner*, Keats's *The Eve of St Agnes*, Masefield's *Reynard the Fox* and Auden's *The Age of Anxiety* have not even been referred to. The American Robert Frost has written a number of excellent poems in the genre, including *Death of the Hired Man*, a wise and moving story told in artfully manipulated blank verse. T. S. Eliot's *The Love Song of J. Alfred Prufrock* and *Portrait of a Lady* are both narratives in which much of the plot is submerged: both resemble novels by Henry James from which the mass of description, comment and dialogue has been pared down to a lyrical quintessence.

As with all other kinds of poetry, the *meaning* of a narrative poem – that is to say its plot or story-line – is of secondary importance to the way in which the poet uses language. The story told may frequently be a familiar, perhaps legendary one, so those feelings of suspense or simple curiosity about how things are going to turn out, which are aroused by a good prose story, are less important to the reader than the pleasure he receives from the glitter of words and images, the haunting cadences of the rhythms, and the sense of mystery which cannot be satisfactorily explained by reference to the events portrayed in the narrative.

The Love Song of J. Alfred Prufrock begins with the surprising, rather surrealistic image of the evening above a great city '. . . spread out against the sky/Like a patient etherised upon a table.' We follow the protagonist of the poem, an indecisive, inadequate male figure approaching middle age, whose life seems without direction and who appears to have reached a crossroads where all choices lead only to further emptiness and ennui; yet he is probed by yearnings for a lost world of instinctive joy and beauty. After a sequence of images of urban triviality imbued with a sense of utter pointlessness and the uneasy sense of mortality, the poem ends with these lines which, with their conventional romanticism of both form and vocabulary, contrast poignantly with all that has gone before:

> I have heard the mermaids singing, each to each.
>
> I do not think that they will sing to me.
>
> I have seen them riding seaward on the waves
> Combing the white hair of the waves blown back
> When the wind blows the water white and black.
>
> We have lingered in the chambers of the sea
> By sea-girls wreathed with seaweed red and brown
> Till human voices wake us, and we drown.

What I have been suggesting is that, when we go to narrative poetry, of whatever kind, the story itself is unlikely to be what draws us towards it nor what remains most powerfully in the consciousness after the poem has been read. With the satirical or didactic poetry of, say, Dryden, Pope and Swift, what enchants is the play of wit, the justness of criticism, the verbal pyrotechnics. From more romantic narrative poems we remember the resonances of language, the visual or auditory imagery, the radiance and the music rather than the events and characters in the story. It is the poetry that we are drawn to rather than the tale, which could have been, and in some cases has already been, told in plain prose. There always lies at the heart of authentic poetry, of whatever kind, a lyrical impulse. In the next chapter, then, we shall look deeper into what constitutes this elusive quality, and ask what we mean by 'lyrical poetry'.

5

LYRICAL POETRY

The word 'lyric' or 'lyrical' has come to cover a considerable range of different kinds of poetry. The term derives from the Greek lyre, a stringed musical instrument used to accompany a singer, and originally it meant simply words intended for singing; but, while many lyrical poems have retained that earlier meaning, by no means all of them would be suitable for musical setting. What distinguishes the lyrical poem – or the lyrical quality in a poem which may not in its entirety be described as a lyric – is a quality of deeply felt personal response to an emotional experience, expressed in rhythmical language, usually employing regular metre and rhyme. Keats's *Ode to a Nightingale* is a lyrical poem, and a very beautiful one, but, because of its comparative length and its complexity of rhythm, thought and imagery, one cannot imagine its being set to music and sung. However, many lyrical poems written during the past hundred years or so, though not composed specifically as songs, are quite suitable for musical setting; indeed, numbers of them have inspired composers to provide music for them. Lyrical poems by Tennyson, Housman and Thomas Hardy have been arranged as delightful songs by, among others, Benjamin Britten, Ralph Vaughan Williams and Gerald Finzi.

The Elizabethans John Dowland and Thomas Campion were both musicians and composers as well as poets, and were thus able to provide musical settings for their own lyrics which had been written for the express purpose of being sung to the accompaniment of the lute; however, few poets since that time have written lyrical poems for which they would regard a musical setting as quite necessary. The composers of pop songs sometimes supply both words and music or, as in the case of Simon and Garfunkel among others, one of the pair writes the music and the other the words. But there is an immense difference between the lyrics of Paul Simon and those of, say, Campion or Dowland. Simon's words function as a kind of pretty verbal decoration which floats on the surface of the melody provided by his partner, and isolated from the music and printed on the page as verse their impoverishment of real feeling, thought or craftsmanship becomes glaringly obvious. A Campion or a Dowland song, such as this one by the latter, can, even without its musical setting, give pleasure as pure poetry:

> Weep you no more, sad fountains;
> What need you flow so fast?
> Look how the snowy mountains
> Heaven's sun doth gently waste.
> But my sun's heavenly eyes
> View not your weeping,
> That now lies sleeping
> Softly, now softly lies
> Sleeping.

> Sleep is a reconciling,
> A rest that peace begets.
> Doth not the sun rise smiling
> When fair at ev'n he sets?
> Rest you then, rest, sad eyes,
> Melt not in weeping
> While she lies sleeping
> Softly, now softly lies
> Sleeping.

There are a number of prescribed poetic forms which lyrical poets may employ, though many lyrics, such as the one by Dowland, are written in verse patterns which are devised by their authors. The **sonnet** is by far the most popular of the prescribed modes and some of the finest lyrical poems in the language have been composed in this form. Though the **ode** was originally, in classical literature, a poem intended for singing, it has come to mean a work in rhymed verse which celebrates the beauty of an animate or inanimate object, a season or even a philosophical idea. Keats's *Ode on a Grecian Urn*, Shelley's *Ode to the West Wind,* and Wordsworth's *Ode: Intimations of Immortality* are all in their different styles splendid poems, but it would be hard to imagine any of them being sung.

The **villanelle** is a set verse form which the English have inherited from the French. It was originally a simple pastoral poem – that is, a short lyrical piece which celebrates the delights of country pleasures, traditionally featuring nymphs and shepherds – but in the hands of twentieth-century writers it has become capable of accommodating material of far greater complexity. The pattern is repetitive and, for English poets whose language is not rich in rhyming words, quite demanding. The villanelle consists of five tercets with a concluding quatrain: The first line is repeated in the sixth and twelfth lines and the third line in the ninth and fifteenth, the two coming together as a rhyming couplet to conclude the poem: an example should make this clear. Here is a fine villanelle by Dylan Thomas, a moving exhortation to his old father to face death, not with resignation but defiance:

> Do not go gentle into that good night,
> Old age should burn and rave at close of day;
> Rage, rage against the dying of the light.
>
> Though wise men at their end know dark is right,
> Because their words had forked no lightning they
> Do not go gentle into that good night.
>
> Good men, the last wave by, crying how bright
> Their frail deeds might have danced in a green bay,
> Rage, rage against the dying of the light.

Wild men who caught and sang the sun in flight,
And learn too late, they grieved it on its way,
Do not go gentle into that good night.

Grave men, near death, who see with blinding sight
Blind eyes could blaze like meteors and be gay,
Rage, rage against the dying of the light.

And you, my father, there on the sad height,
Curse, bless, me now with your fierce tears, I pray.
Do not go gentle into that good night.
Rage, rage against the dying of the light.

Other prescribed lyric forms include the **rondeau, ballade** (not to be confused with the plain ballad), and **sestina.** However they are used comparatively infrequently by English poets and, when they are employed, the results are of mainly technical interest and offer relatively little to the reader who goes to poetry for pleasure or consolation.

Lyrical poetry, then, covers an enormously wide range of verse forms and subject matter. The most common themes are those opposed, yet immensely fruitful, presences in all romantic art, Love and Death. Other favourite concerns are celebrations of natural beauty, the weather and seasons, and art itself – anything, in fact, which stirs the poet's emotions. On the subject of love, both sacred and profane, it is probably safe to say that more lyrical poetry has been written than on any other theme. Love lyrics in the English language range from simple songs celebrating the joy of fulfilment, through laments over the inconstancy or indifference of the beloved, to subtle analyses of the nature of love itself.

An early anonymous love lyric, written about five hundred years ago and only four lines in length, retains all of its power to move through its naked simplicity of utterance and the universality of the feeling which has prompted the poet to write:

O Western wind, when wilt thou blow
    That the small rain down can rain?
Christ, that my love were in my arms,
    And I in my bed again.

This sense of separation and the hunger for the presence of the loved one is repeated throughout English poetry, and variations upon the theme are still being written to the present day. Here, for example, is an even shorter poem by the twentieth-century writer Robert Graves which, though more intellectualised, is still essentially a cry from the heart and deals with the same theme of absence from, and yearning for, the object of the poet's love:

> Black drinks the sun and draws all colours to it.
> I am bleached white, my truant love. Come back,
> And stain me with intensity of black.

While the theme of separation is a fairly common one in English love poetry there are at least as many poems which are direct celebrations of the virtues and charms of the beloved, and the best of these transcend the merely personal and temporal and become tributes to the eternal qualities which the poet extols at a particular time and place in a particular woman. Ben Jonson (1572–1637) wrote a glorious catalogue of his mistress's attractions in a work entitled *A Celebration of Charis in Ten Lyrick Pieces,* and the images he presents in this, the final stanza of the fourth piece, have lost none of their power to delight during the intervening four centuries:

> Have you seene but a bright Lillie grow,
> Before rude hands have touch'd it?
> Have you mark'd but the fall o'the Snow
> Before the soyle hath smutch'd it?
> Have you felt the wooll o'the Bever?
> Or Swans Downe ever?
> Or have smelt o'the bud o'the Brier?
> Or the Nard i'the fire?
> Or have tasted the bag o'the Bee?
> O so white! O so soft! O so sweet is she!

As in life itself, so in poetry, unrequited love is a familiar experience and it is a subject which has been treated by English poets in a variety of ways. Edmund Waller (1606–1687) wrote a fine lyric, *Go, Lovely Rose,* in which he compares the lady he desires to the rose which he is sending to her with the poem. However, the purpose of his message is not simply to flatter her: the rose is certainly an emblem reflecting her beauty but it is also a *memento mori*, a reminder of the brevity of youth, beauty and life itself, and the poem is in fact a plea that she should give herself to him while she is still desired.

> Go, lovely Rose!
> Tell her, that wastes her time and me,
>   That now she knows,
> When I resemble her to thee,
> How sweet and fair she seems to be.
>
> Tell her that's young
> And shuns to have her graces spied,
>   That hadst thou sprung
> In deserts, where no men abide,
> Thou must have uncommended died.
>
> Small is the worth
> Of beauty from the light retired.
>   Bid her come forth,
> Suffer herself to be desired,
> And not blush so to be admired.
>
> Then die! that she,
> The common fate of all things rare
>   May read in thee:
> How small a part of time they share
> That are so wondrous sweet and fair.

During the sixteenth and seventeenth centuries a tradition of composing graceful love lyrics developed to the point at which many of these, while exquisitely wrought, began to seem over-contrived and to be making use of images that were not true expressions of passionate feeling but gestures as formal and meaningless as those of dancers in a quadrille. But, as almost always happens at moments like these in the history of literature, a few tough-minded, intelligent, undeceivable writers came along and mocked the orthodoxies of the moment. One of these was Sir John Suckling, a younger contemporary of Waller, a fine poet but not the kind of man to adopt a sycophantic or wheedling pose in the presence of an

unrelenting lady whose favours he was courting. In the following poem the tone is one of good-natured, robust impati-
ence with all tiresome attitudinising, whether in love or
poetry:

> Why so pale and wan, fond lover?
> > Prithee, why so pale?
> Will, when looking well can't move her,
> > Looking ill prevail?
> > Prithee, why so pale?
>
> Why so dull and mute, young sinner?
> > Prithee, why so mute?
> Will, when speaking well can't win her,
> > Saying nothing do't?
> > Prithee, why so mute?
>
> Quit, quit for shame! This will not move;
> > This cannot take her.
> If of herself she will not love,
> > Nothing can make her.
> > The devil take her!

That little explosion of exasperation at the end is sympatheti-
cally comic, and the elements of humour and wit, while seem-
ing to belong to the satiric rather than the lyric mode, are in
fact not uncommon in lyrical poetry, especially that of the
seventeenth century. Andrew Marvell's *To His Coy Mistress* is
a brilliant, witty, tender and passionate poem, charged with
the verbal music and unexpected conjunctions of disparate
phenomena which are the hallmarks of the best lyrics; Herrick's slighter but delicately constructed love poems are,
almost without exception, good-humoured and frequently
witty, and John Donne's love lyrics are unrivalled for their
mixture of personal feeling, originality and deployment of
astonishing yet apt metaphors.

Donne (1572–1631) in his earlier years wrote a good
deal of satirical verse and poems that were erotic and worldly,
but in 1615 he took Anglican orders and for the last ten years
of his life he was Dean of St Paul's, preaching many of his
magnificent sermons before King Charles I. His religious
poetry possesses a similar strength of feeling to that shown by

his profane love poetry, and in one of his Holy Sonnets his petition for the gift of divine love is expressed in terms of earthly erotic love, working through a series of apparently contradictory statements to the final splendid paradoxes of the last three lines:

> Batter my heart, three-personed God; for you
> As yet but knock, breathe, shine, and seek to mend.
> That I may rise and stand, o'erthrow me and bend
> Your force to break, blow, burn and make me new.
> I, like an usurped town, to another due,
> Labour to admit you, but, oh, to no end;
> Reason, your viceroy in me, me should defend,
> But is captived and proves weak or untrue.
> Yet dearly I love you and would be loved fain,
> But am betrothed unto your enemy:
> Divorce me, untie or break that knot again,
> Take me to you, imprison me, for I,
> Except you enthrall me, never shall be free,
> Nor ever chaste, except you ravish me.

The religious lyric is very often a love poem in which the desire has been spiritualised and redirected to a supernatural object, though it is not often expressed in such frankly erotic terms as in Donne's sonnet. George Herbert, whose poem *Prayer* was quoted in Chapter 2, addressed many of his lyrics to a God whom he clearly regarded anthropomorphically in the simplest human terms, and these poems possess a candour and purity of thought and vision that should touch the heart of any reader, whatever the nature of his religious views. This tradition of the simple religious lyrical poem which draws for its imagery upon the ordinary objects and experiences of daily life has been continued to the present time.

One of the greatest and most original poets England has produced, Gerard Manley Hopkins, was born in 1844 and while at Oxford he became converted to the Church of Rome. He later became a Jesuit priest, and for the last five years of his life (1844–1889) he was Professor of Greek at Dublin University. A number of his sonnets deal with the agonies of a committed Christian who is in danger of losing his faith, and they dramatise his spiritual struggle with powerful authenticity. But, elsewhere, he has rejoiced in the certainties of Christian belief and praised God through celebrating the splendour of His creation, the landscape, seasons, flora and fauna, not forgetting Man himself. Hopkins was a technical innovator of the first importance, experimenting with a type of metre which he called 'sprung-rhythm', based on the stresses of natural speech rather than on a count of syllables, and his influence on subsequent poetry in the English language has been far-reaching. Some of his lyrics are, however, perfectly traditional in form, though all are distinguished by his sensitive ear and instinct for the rhythms and images which convey precisely the effects he wishes to communicate in terms of meaning, sound and feeling:

A Nun Takes the Veil

I have desired to go
   Where springs not fail,
To fields where flies no sharp and sided hail,
   And a few lilies blow.

And I have asked to be
   Where no storms come,
Where the green swell is in the havens dumb
   And out of the swing of the sea.

Notice how, in that last line, the heavy stresses on 'out', 'swing' and 'sea', the one iambic foot followed by two anapaests and the final long vowel sound in 'sea' all transmit the sense of rising and falling on the swell of the waves and then moving into the peaceful stillness as the poem ends, that calm seclusion which is, in a spiritual sense, the subject of the poem.

Opposed to, or sometimes in reconciliation with, the affirmations of erotic and divine love in English poetry are the darker but no less resonant poems inspired by death itself, or by the awareness of its presence which mocks, yet paradoxically gives value to, all human striving. John Donne, writing from the security of his faith in the immortality of the soul, wrote this magnificent sonnet addressed to death:

Death, be not proud, though some have callèd thee
Mighty and dreadful, for thou art not so;
For those whom thou think'st thou dost overthrow
Die not, poor Death; nor yet canst thou kill me.
From Rest and Sleep, which but thy picture be,
Much pleasure; then from thee much more must flow;
And soonest our best men with thee do go –
Rest of their bones and souls' delivery!
Thou'rt slave to fate, chance, kings, and
                              desperate men,
And dost with poison, war, and sickness dwell;
And poppy or charms can make us sleep as well
And better than thy stroke. Why swell'st thou then?
One short sleep past, we wake eternally,
And Death shall be no more: Death, thou shalt die!

Donne conducts a rational argument in this poem, but the power and memorability of the lines do not depend on the reader's acceptance of his case but on the rich orchestration of the language, the surge and flow of the rhythms and the triumphantly percussive last line.

     Over three hundred years later Dylan Thomas wrote a poem which takes the same subject – the defiance of death's omnipotence – but approached it from the viewpoint, not of orthodox Christian belief, but from that of a pantheistic notion of the continuity of life in the earth, plants and waters of the creation. Nevertheless I do not regard it as fanciful to recognise distinct echoes of Donne in the powerful thrust and beat of these lines, the strong alliteration and assonances, though there is a quality in the diction, rhythm and imagery that is distinctively the young Welsh poet's own.

And death shall have no dominion.
Dead men naked they shall be one
With the man in the wind and the west moon;
When their bones are picked clean and the clean
                              bones gone,
They shall have stars at elbow and foot;
Though they go mad they shall be sane,
Though they sink through the sea they shall rise
                              again;
Though lovers be lost love shall not;
And death shall have no dominion.

And death shall have no dominion.
Under the windings of the sea
They lying long shall not die windily;
Twisting on racks when sinews give way,
Strapped to a wheel, yet they shall not break;
Faith in their hands shall snap in two,
And the unicorn evils run them through;
Split all ends up they shan't crack;
And death shall have no dominion.

And death shall have no dominion.
No more may gulls cry at their ears
Or waves break loud on the seashores;
Where blew a flower may a flower no more
Lift its head to the blows of the rain;
Though they be mad and dead as nails,
Heads of the characters hammer through daisies;
Break in the sun till the sun breaks down,
And death shall have no dominion.

Those two lyrical poems treated death in a generalised way, each attempting to minimise its malign power. More personal lyrics commemorating particular deaths offer us a different, sadder music, especially when they deal with someone deeply loved, and most poignantly of all when the subject is a child. Ben Jonson has written most movingly on the death of one of his children:

On my First Sonne

Farewell, thou child of my right hand, and joy;
    My sinne was too much hope of thee, lov'd boy,
Seven yeeres tho'wert lent to me, and I thee pay,
    Exacted by thy fate, on the just day.
O, could I loose all father, now. For why
    Will man lament the state he should envie?
To have so soone scap'd worlds, and fleshes rage,
    And, if no other miserie, yet age?
Rest in soft peace, and, ask'd say here doth lye
    BEN. JONSON his best piece of *poetrie*.
For whose sake, hence-forth, all his vowes be such,
    As what he loves may never like too much.

What, for this reader, lifts the little poem above the level of more conventional elegies is the surprising but entirely apt use of the phrase 'his best piece of *poetrie*'. The simplicity of the phrasing is wholly appropriate: for a professional and totally dedicated poet, such as Jonson, his best poem would be the thing he valued above all others. The unaffected directness of referring to his dead child in these terms is infinitely more convincing and touching than any more elaborate expression of grief would be.

The same kind of simplicty and refusal to indulge in rhetorical flourishes may be found in Wordsworth's little elegy for Lucy:

> She dwelt among the untrodden ways
>> Beside the springs of Dove,
> A maid whom there were none to praise
>> And very few to love:
>
> A violet by a mossy stone
>> Half hidden from the eye!
> – Fair as a star, when only one
>> Is shining in the sky.
>
> She lived unknown, and few could know
>> When Lucy ceased to be;
> But she is in her grave, and, oh,
>> The difference to me!

The understatement of that last line conveys a depth of feeling which would be reduced by a more grandiose use of language. Perhaps its effectiveness may be better seen when the poem is compared with another short elegiac lyric where the poet is clearly attempting to reach the reader's emotions through a fairly complex development of contrasting images. Here is Christina Rossetti's (1830–1894) *A Dirge:*

> Why were you born when the snow was falling?
> You should have come to the cuckoo's calling,
> Or when the grapes are green in the cluster,
> Or, at least, when lithe swallows muster
>> For their far off flying
>> From summer dying.

> Why did you die when the lambs were cropping?
> You should have died at the apples' dropping,
> When the grasshopper comes to trouble,
> And the wheat-fields are sodden stubble,
>> For all winds go sighing
>> For sweet things dying.

That is a quite neatly composed lyric but its conscious artistry invites disbelief in the authenticity of the emotion that the poet wishes to convey. One feels that the author is rather pleased with having written an effective piece of verse, and the second line in the second stanza gives the game away: 'You should have died . . .' says Christina Rossetti, as if true grief could conceivably be mitigated by the dead person's having chosen an appropriately autumnal setting for his or her departure.

This is not to say, however, that an intricate and eloquent style cannot be employed by the elegiac lyricist. For writing a personal elegy I suggest that chastity of language and simplicity of imagery are almost always the most effective means of transmitting profound feeling, but in the more generalised poem dealing with death, such as Thomas Gray's *Elegy Written in a Country Churchyard,* the variety and richness of metaphor and rhetoric are important factors contributing to its complete success. In the twentieth century Wilfred Owen wrote a short lament, in sonnet form, for the dead, or those who were doomed to die, in the First World War. Here the poet makes a bitterly ironic identification of the orthodox Christian burial rites, with their bells, prayers, choirs and candles, and the devilish rituals of battle, artillery and rifle fire, the wailing of shells and the cry of bugles; the poem is a harsh indictment of both the appalling futility and waste of war and the irrelevance and hypocrisy of organised religion in time of war, but it is also a profoundly moving tribute to both the dead and to those who unobtrusively and sincerely mourn them.

Anthem for Doomed Youth

What passing-bells for these who die as cattle?
Only the monstrous anger of the guns.

Only the stuttering rifles' rapid rattle
Can patter out their hasty orisons.
No mockeries for them; no prayers nor bells,
Nor any voice of mourning save the choirs, –
The shrill, demented choirs of wailing shells;
And bugles calling for them from sad shires.
What candles may be held to speed them all?
Not in the hands of boys, but in their eyes
Shall shine the holy glimmers of good-byes.
The pallor of girls' brows shall be their pall;
Their flowers the tenderness of patient minds,
And each slow dusk a drawing-down of blinds.

Edward Thomas who, like Owen, was killed in the First World War, did not write much verse which made direct reference to the conflict itself; he was primarily a poet who drew his inspiration from the English countryside, the vagaries of the weather and seasons, flowers, plants and birds. His lyrical poems – and almost everything he wrote was essentially lyrical – are much more than word-pictures or simple tributes to their subjects. Beneath the surface of the objects and events presented are other presences: a sense of unease, loneliness, anxiety, hope and fear. He had the great poet's gift for condensing almost inexhaustible meanings into very few lines, the gift, in Keat's words to Shelley, of loading 'every rift with ore':

Thaw

Over the land freckled with snow half-thawed
The speculating rooks at their nests cawed
And saw from elm-tops, delicate as flower of grass,
What we below could not see, Winter pass.

At first glance this might seem merely a charming little picture of a snow-covered landscape observed from a bird's-eye view as the thaw begins. But a closer look at the poem soon reveals to eye, ear and mind that it is considerably more than a pleasing watercolour or snapshot. First the sounds, the musical effect, are contrived with great skill: notice how the first syllable of 'freckled' and 'speculating' rhyme internally, and the harsh 'k' sounds of these two words, when linked with 'rooks' and 'cawed', mimic the cries of the birds. The view is that of the rooks on the elm-tops, but with the description 'delicate as flowers of grass' the viewpoint shifts to the earth and we are looking up at the trees. Humankind is too close to the ground to see the gradual processes of the thaw and, as Thomas is implying, in order to see things clearly we must distance ourselves from whatever we are viewing. Paradoxically the poet, through the exercise of imagination, by *becoming* in the first two-and-a-half lines the rooks in the elm-tops, can see winter pass. So this simple and very pleasing little lyric, besides presenting an accurate picture of a winter landscape, tells us something about the working of the poet's imagination and the need for the artist to distance himself from his subject if he is successfully to comprehend it.

Not all lyrics which take for their subject the countryside, weather and seasons are as concentrated as Thomas's *Thaw*, but most use their subject matter to symbolise something beyond simple physical appearances and sensations. Even the works of a poet like John Clare, a simple countryman, usually contain something more than accurate pictures of rural life in the early nineteenth century. Clare was born in 1793, the son of a Northamptonshire farm labourer, and he himself was employed on the land for most of his working life. He met with some literary success early in his career when he published *Poems Descriptive of Rural Life* in 1820 and *The Village Minstrel* in 1821, but he was declared insane in 1837 and ended his days in Northampton County Asylum. His nature poems are packed with well-observed detail and a strong but unsentimental compassion for all forms of wild life. In *Winter Morning* the physical details are presented and no generalised comment is made; nevertheless the reader senses Clare's sympathy with the 'labouring men' who must work through the freezing day before they can enjoy the brief and limited comfort of the fireside.

> The morning wakens with the lumping flails,
> Chilly and cold; the early-rising clown
> Hurkles along and blows his finger nails;
> Icicles from the cottage eaves hang down,
> Which peeping children wish for in their play.
> The field, once clad in autumn's russet brown,
> Spreads from the eye its circle far away

In one huge sheet of snow; from the white wood
The crows all silent seek the dreary fens,
And starnels blacken through the air in crowds;
The sheep stand bleating in their turnip pen
And loathe their frozen food; while labouring men
Button their coats more close from angry clouds
And wish for night and its snug fire agen.

Poems of place and weather do not, of course, always confine
themselves to rural scenes. Many poets, especially since the
Industrial Revolution, have been attracted by urban life as a
subject for verse and, long before London became the sprawl-
ing metropolis we know today, Wordsworth wrote this fine
tranquil description of the view from *Westminster Bridge:*

Earth has not anything to show more fair:
Dull would he be of soul who could pass by
A sight so touching in its majesty:
This city now doth, like a garment, wear
The beauty of the morning; silent, bare,
Ships, towers, domes, theatres, and temples lie
Open unto the fields, and to the sky:
All bright and glittering in the smokeless air.
Never did sun more beautifully steep
In his first splendour, valley, rock, or hill;
Ne'er saw I, never felt, a calm so deep!
The river glideth at his own sweet will:
Dear God! the very houses seem asleep;
And all that mighty heart is lying still!

Among poets of the twentieth century W. H. Auden, Dylan
Thomas, Louis MacNeice and many others have written effective lyrical verse using the images of metropolitan life, and
more recent writers such as Tony Harrison, a Leeds man, and
Philip Larkin, who lives and works in Hull, have used provincial settings for excellent lyrics or for poems with a strong
lyrical pulse. Here is Larkin's *Arrivals, Departures,* a haunting
evocation of the seaport with its melancholy sounds of ships'
horns used as a metaphor for the unpredictable vacillations of
fortune and for birth and death themselves.

This town has docks where channel boats come
sidling;
Tame water lanes, tall sheds, the traveller sees
(His bag of samples knocking at his knees),
And hears, still under slackened engines gliding,
His advent blurted to the morning shore.

And we, barely recalled from sleep there, sense
Arrivals lowing in a doleful distance –
Horny dilemmas at the gate once more.
Come and choose wrong, the cry, *come and choose
wrong;*
And so we rise. At night again they sound,

Calling the traveller now, the outward bound:
O not for long, the cry, *O not for long –*
And we are nudged from comfort, never knowing
How safely we may disregard their blowing,
Or if, this night, happiness too is going.

Some of the poems I have quoted in this chapter may seem to
have departed a considerable distance from the basic definition of 'lyrical' as descriptive of verse suitable for musical setting, yet I think that every one does to some degree offer that
'singing' quality, a resonance that is a result of the words, their
conjunction and juxtaposition, together with their meanings
and associations, yet seems to exist independently of them as
an abstract melody. You can 'hear' such poems, like a half-
recollected tune, without being able to remember all of the
words. I believe that many of these poems would present
serious difficulties to a composer who was commissioned to
set them, and I cannot accept that a poem such as *Anthem for
Doomed Youth* benefits from musical accompaniment, though
it has, in fact, been set by Benjamin Britten in his *War
Requiem*. Most lyrical poetry provides its own verbal music,
the modulated cadences of speech, and the accompaniment of
non-verbal, instrumental music might well be an obtrusive
irrelevance.

However, the musical associations of the lyric are still
important and the lyrical poem, in its simplest form, that of the
song, carol or incantation, demonstrates this fact inescapably.
Shakespeare's songs, such as the one from the play *Cymbeline*

– from which I give here the first two verses – could be just as
effectively sung as spoken:

> Fear no more the heat o' the sun,
>   Nor the furious winter's rages;
> Thou thy worldly task hast done,
>   Home art gone, and ta'en thy wages;
> Golden lads and girls all must,
> As chimney-sweepers, come to dust.
>
> Fear no more the frown o' the great,
>   Thou art past the tyrant's stroke:
> Care no more to clothe and eat;
>   To thee the reed is as the oak:
> The sceptre, learning, physic, must
> All follow this, and come to dust.

The influence of such early songs has never been lost from
lyrical poetry and its presence may be detected or felt even in
poems which are not strictly lyrical. In this little lyric by A. E.
Housman (1859–1936) the tone is closer to that of the Elizabethan poets than to what we commonly think of as the idiom of
our own time:

> With rue my heart is laden
>   For golden friends I had,
> For many a rose-lipt maiden
>   And many a lightfoot lad.
>
> By brooks too broad for leaping
>   The lightfoot boys are laid;
> The rose-lipt girls are sleeping
>   In fields where roses fade.

In this short poem the family resemblance to the Elizabethan
song is very marked indeed, so much so that one might protest
that Housman is merely imitating his great predecessors. If
this is to be conceded, then it can only be said that he does it
so supremely well that we should be grateful, yet a valid critical point has been made. While the subject matter of poetry
does not change any more than the eternal human preoccupations in life itself change – love, hope, hate, ambition, envy,
jealousy, the quest for truth and justice, praise of the good and

beautiful, and condemnation of the evil and destructive – poetry should reflect the changes in language and society that have occurred in the author's lifetime, so even the 'timeless' beauty of the pure lyric should be able, as Shakespeare's songs were able, to reflect the spirit of his age and the genius of the spoken language of that particular time. Consider the following *Song:*

> Now sleeps the crimson petal, now the white;
> Nor waves the cypress in the palace walk;
> Nor winks the gold fin in the porphyry font:
> The fire-fly wakens: waken thou with me.
>
> Now droops the milk white peacock like a ghost,
> And like a ghost she glimmers on to me.
>
> Now lies the Earth all Danae to the stars,
> And all thy heart lies open unto me.
> Now slides the silent meteor on, and leaves
> A shining furrow, as thy thoughts in me.
>
> Now folds the lily all her sweetness up,
> And slips into the bosom of the lake:
> So fold thyself, my dearest, thou, and slip
> Into my bosom and be lost in me.

This beautiful poem by Alfred, Lord Tennyson could reasonably claim to embody all of the traditional lyric qualities. It is concerned with deep feeling, the emotion of passionate love, the language is sonorous, the rhythms delightful, the imagery simple but vivid. The poem offers its own music, yet it would certainly be suitable for setting by a composer and performance by musician and singer. But, unlike the Housman lyric, it is entirely original. We hear Tennyson's voice and it is the voice of mid-Victorian man, not imitating the tones of the Elizabethans but speaking in the idiom and expressing the spirit of his own day. The furnishings of the poem – the cypress in the palace walk, the goldfish in the porphyry font, peacock, lily, lake and so on are familiar from the paintings of the Pre-Raphaelites. Technically the poem owes little to examples from the past. In fact it is remarkably innovatory. Unlike almost all lyrics it does not, in the conventional sense, rhyme. The regular repetitions of 'me' are not of course strictly rhymes but function in the same way as orthodox rhymes would, as, less obtrusively, the internal repetitions of 'waken/ wakened', 'ghost', 'lies', 'fold/folds', 'slips/slip' and 'bosom', combined with the subtly deployed assonances and alliteration, all work together to create the desired dream-like effect which precise rhyme would almost certainly have dispelled.

I should like to end this chapter with a descriptive lyrical poem by a fine living American poet, Richard Wilbur – one which will, I hope, clearly demonstrate the point that, however traditional in spirit, the best poetry is never merely imitative of literature of the past but, in its vocabulary and speech rhythms, unequivocally of its time. The subject of the poem is timeless – a frozen river thawing, symbolising regeneration in unexpected places and circumstances, the continuous mystery and magic of existence – but the language and imagery belong to the twentieth century.

A Glance from the Bridge

Letting the eye descend from reeking stack
And black façade to where the river goes,
You see the freeze has started in to crack
(As if the city squeezed it in a vice),
And here and there the limbering water shows,
And gulls colonial on the sullied ice.

Some rise and braid their glidings, white and spare,
Or sweep the hemmed-in river up and down,
Making a litheness in the barriered air,
And through the town the freshening water swirls
As if an ancient whore undid her gown
And showed a body almost like a girl's.

6

THE
CHANGING
FACE OF
POETRY

I made the point in the previous chapter that authentic poetry reflects the spirit of the time in which it is composed, and that there is a direct relationship between the cadences and speech patterns of the common language of the day and the language employed by poets. This relationship is not, of course, a mirror image or duplication; although common speech often contains the uncut stones of poetic imagery and the rhythm of its verbal music, a transcription of ordinary conversation would obviously not produce poetry. The poet selects from the rhythms and locutions of spoken language the cadences and word combinations which satisfy his ear and embody whatever feeling and thought he wishes to convey. The poem is not a transcribing of speech but, ideally, a perfecting of it. The poet says about life, love, and death what we would all say if our tongues were miraculously given the power of supreme eloquence and precision of expression. So poetic language, while remaining in touch with the speech of its time, must be prepared to distance itself and, when necessary, assert its right to behave in ways that would be quite strange to the man or woman who is simply striving

to communicate commonplace desires, ideas, needs and information for practical purposes; on the other hand it must not with-
draw too far from its idiomatic origins or it will become artificial,
remote and lifeless.

For a full appreciation of the poetry of a past era we
need some knowledge of both the social forces at work during
that period, and of the state of the language of ordinary intercourse and its relations with the literary style or styles prevailing. In a sense it is true that great poetry, like all great art,
transcends its time and becomes permanently significant and
moving beyond any temporal or spatial limits, but it is also
true that, in all but a very few cases, an awareness of the historical background to the poem is necessary before it can be
fully appreciated. The twentieth-century reader of even as
great and universal a poet as Shakespeare is aware of a voice
employing a vocabulary and linguistic patterns which he would
not expect to find in the work of one of his own contemporaries. Quite simply, no twentieth-century poet would begin a
poem as Shakespeare begins this splendid sonnet, of which I
quote here the first eight lines:

> Shall I compare thee to a Summer's day?
> Thou art more lovely and more temperate:
> Rough winds do shake the darling buds of May
> And Summer's lease hath all too short a date:
> Sometimes too hot the eye of heaven shines,
> And often is his gold complexion dimmed,
> And every fair from fair sometime declines,
> By chance, or nature's changing course
> untrimmed:. . .

The modern reader may enjoy this without much sense of having to switch his receptive powers on to a different
wavelength from the one on which he will receive, for instance, the sonnet *Who's Who*, by the twentieth-century poet
W. H. Auden, which begins:

> A shilling life will give you all the facts:
> How father beat him, how he ran away,
> What were the struggles of his youth, what acts
> Made him the greatest figure of his day:

Of how he fought, fished, hunted, worked all night,
Though giddy, climbed new mountains; named a sea:
Some of the last researchers even write
Love made him weep pints like you and me.

A switch, though probably an unconscious one, will neverthe-less be made.

Perhaps the most obvious purely verbal difference is the use of the second person pronouns 'thee' and 'thou' and the archaic verb forms of 'art' and 'hath', but there are also more subtle differences of word order or syntax. In the third line of the Shakespeare sonnet the word 'do' would be omitted in modern speech or writing, and in the last four lines quoted the syntax follows a form closer to Latin sentence structure than to modern English, with the verb appearing at the end of each clause: in the present century one would say, or write, 'Some-times the eye of heaven shines too hot', 'And every fair some-times declines from fair', and 'Untrimmed by chance or nature's changing course'. The syntax of the Auden lines fol-lows the speech patterns we would use today; there are no inversions of word order and the phrasing is colloquial, though the iambic metre is as regular as Shakespeare's.

In order to help readers to enjoy poetry of different periods the following pages contain a simplified and neces-sarily superficial but, I hope, useful account of the evolution of poetic forms and practice as they have been developed or modified from the time of Chaucer in the fourteenth century to the late twentieth century.

Chaucer to Spenser

Geoffrey Chaucer was born in or about 1340, almost three hundred years after the Norman Conquest. Before the suc-cessful invasion of England by French-speakers in 1066 there existed an indigenous literature in this island, mainly in verse form, the most famous single work being the Anglo-Saxon epic *Beowulf*, but the language spoken by the natives of England and the language of *Beowulf*, which was sung by the minstrels or 'scops' (the smiths of song), and finally written down by an unknown monk in the tenth century, was not a primitive form of the English we speak today but an entirely different language with its own vocabulary and grammatical structures. For almost a century after the Norman Conquest the official language of England was French, though Old English, or Anglo-Saxon, continued to be spoken by the natives and their descendants; gradually the two languages fused and a new tongue, known as Middle English, evolved. This was the language that Chaucer did so much to bring to maturity, welding the French and English elements into a fluent unity.

In the century and a half that followed the death of Chaucer English poetry developed a rich flexibility and we can observe the shifting balance between the wish to aim at the classical virtues of elegance and control, based upon a study of Latin and later European models, and the impulse to remain essentially English and make a rougher but stirring music from the rhythms of the local vernacular, the anonymous songs and ballads, the tough muscle and sinew of the spoken tongue itself.

John Skelton (1460–1529) was a poet who, though a formidable classical scholar and tutor to Prince Henry, who was to become Henry VIII, regarded with impatient contempt the tendency of English poets to look to classical or contemporary foreign literature for nourishment and formal guidance, and his own work is obstinately colloquial, rough-hewn and racy. His favourite metre was a vigorous, profusely rhyming short line of two or three stresses, and his language always showed a marked preference for words of Anglo-Saxon rather than French or Latin origin. He is the least abstract of poets, revelling in the names of physical objects and creatures, as is shown in these lines from *To Mistress Isabel Pennell*. A few of the words may be unfamiliar – 'Reflaring rosabel' means redolent rosebud, 'rosary' is a rose bush, 'nept' is mint, 'jelofer' gillyflower and 'Ennewèd' is refreshed.

> By Saint Mary, my lady,
> Your mammy and your daddy
> Brought forth a goodly baby!

**Chaucer to
Spenser**

My maiden Isabel,
Reflaring rosabel.
The fragrant camomel;
The ruddy rosary,
The sovereign rosemary,
The pretty strawberry;
The columbine, the nept,
The jelofer well set,
The proper violet:
Ennewèd your colour
Is like the daisy flower
After the April shower;
Star of the morrow gray,
The blossom on the spray,
The freshest flower of May;
Maidenly demure,
Of womanhood the lure;
Wherefore, I make you sure,
It were an heavenly health,
It were an endless wealth,
A life for God himself,
To hear this nightingale
Among the birdies small
Warbling in the vale,
'Dug, dug,
Jug, jug,
Good year and good luck!'
With Chuck, chuck, chuck, chuck!'

In the work of Sir Thomas Wyatt (1503–1542) we find a far greater variety and sophistication of form than in Skelton, though despite his wide travelling and reading in other languages, and his interest in developing the scope of English verse, he remained essentially an English country squire, fond of rural pursuits and of the native vernacular tradition in his country's literature. He is not to be confused with his son, Sir Thomas Wyatt the Younger, one of the leaders of the 1554 revolt intended to prevent the marriage of Queen Mary to Philip of Spain, who was executed in that year.

Wyatt the poet was educated at St John's College, Cambridge, and subsequently acted for Henry VIII as ambassador in France, Spain, Italy and Portugal, taking advantage of his travels to extend his knowledge of other languages and

of the literary forms being developed on the Continent. It was
Wyatt who, with Henry Howard, Earl of Surrey, brought the
sonnet form to England from Italy, and he experimented
widely in other verse forms imported from abroad. He became
the lover of Anne Boleyn in or around 1525 and there is no
doubt that a number of his love poems are inspired by his passion for her. In 1527 Anne became the mistress of the King,
and Wyatt prudently withdrew his rival claim, but it is clear
from what he afterwards wrote that her rejection of him,
which was indirectly to bring her to such a dreadful end on the
scaffold, wounded him deeply. The pain and bitterness he
experienced is poignantly expressed in this beautiful poem, in
which the spelling has been modernised:

Chaucer to
Spenser

> They flee from me, that sometime did me seek
> With naked foot, stalking in my chamber.
> I have seen them gentle, tame, and meek,
> That now are wild, and do not remember
> That sometime they put themselves in danger
> To take bread at my hand; and now they range
> Busily seeking with a continual change.
>
> Thanked be fortune it hath been otherwise
> Twenty times better; but once, in special,
> In thin array, after a pleasant guise,
> When her loose gown from her shoulders did fall,
> And she me caught in her arms long and small,
> Therewith all sweetly did me kiss
> And softly said, 'Dear heart, how like you this?'
>
> It was no dream; I lay broad waking:
> But all is turned, thorough my gentleness,
> Into a strange fashion of forsaking;
> And I have leave to go of her goodness,
> And she also to use newfangleness.
> But since that I so kindly am served,
> I would fain know what she hath deserved.

The experiments in classical and more recent continental
verse forms so resourcefully performed by Wyatt and Surrey
were used and developed by such gifted poets as Thomas
Sackville, Earl of Dorset (1536–1608), George Gascoigne
(1542–1577) and Sir Edward Dyer (1540–1607), all of whom

Chaucer to
Spenser

both responded and contributed to that gradual flowering of the English language which was to reach unparalleled splendour in the works of the great Elizabethans.

Sir Philip Sidney (1554–1586) was probably the most influential, amd certainly one of the most gifted, poets of his generation. He wrote with brilliant fluency in almost every prescribed lyrical form, and in his work we may easily detect a greater confidence and elegance than in that of any of his predecessors. He was educated at Shrewsbury and Christchurch, Oxford, and he travelled extensively in Europe. He was a friend of Edmund Spenser, who dedicated to him his *Shepheards Calender,* and he was a member of the Areopagus, a literary club whose main function was to encourage the naturalisation into vernacular English of the classical metres of antiquity. In the service of Queen Elizabeth I he volunteered to fight against the Spanish and was mortally wounded at Zutphen in the Netherlands. Unlike many popular anecdotes featuring historical figures, the story of his passing a cup of water, as he lay dying, to another wounded man with the words, 'Thy necessity is greater than mine' is quite true.

His chief works are the *Arcadia,* a prose romance, and *Astrophel and Stella,* a series of sonnets in which Sidney is supposed to have expressed his love for Penelope Devereux, daughter of the first Earl of Essex, who was married against her will to Lord Rich. He wrote the first work of literary criticism in English, the *Apologie for Poetrie* or *Defence of Poesie.*

In the following typical and well-known sonnet from *Astrophel and Stella* you will, I am sure, recognise that a new assurance and verbal dexterity had been introduced by Sidney into English poetry.

Come, Sleep, O Sleep, the certain knot of peace,
The baiting-place of wit, the balm of woe,
The poor man's wealth, the prisoner's release,
The indifferent judge between the high and low;
With shield proof shield me from out the press
Of these fierce darts Despair at me doth throw:
O make me in those civil wars to cease;
I will good tribute pay, if thou do so.
Take thou of me smooth pillows, sweetest bed,

A chamber deaf to noise and blind to light,
A rosy garland and a seary head;
And if these things, as being thine by right,
Move not thy heavy grace, thou shalt in me,
Livelier than elsewhere, Stella's image see.

If Sidney had not shown beyond dispute that English poetry, for variety, richness and elegance of form, had at least equalled the finest work being produced anywhere in Europe, his friend Edmund Spenser (1552–1599) removed any possible doubt. But Spenser achieved more than this. He was, and probably always has been, a less popular poet than Sidney, if only because his major work, *The Faerie Queene,* is so enormously long and complex in its design and intentions. The production of graceful sonnets and other lyrical forms celebrating or lamenting the triumphs and disappointments of romantic love was too modest an ambition for a man of Spenser's temperament and accomplishments. He was resolved to write a great epic poem which would celebrate the achievements and chequered history of England, a poem which, at the same time, would be an allegory of good and evil and would further glorify the English language itself.

The Faerie Queene is a work which today is read in its entirety only by specialists, but the ordinary reader may find many passages of power and beauty expressed in such magnificently wrought language that he will not be surprised to learn that Spenser has been called 'the poet's poet'. His influence on Milton, Keats and Tennyson was greater than that of any other writer and he was the first English poet to produce a work on the grand scale that could stand beside the great romantic epic, *Orlando Furioso,* of the Italian Ariosto (1474–1533).

With *The Faerie Queene* English poetry had risen to a new and exalted level, though most modern readers will prefer to take his reputation on trust and they are likely to prefer the less demanding *Amoretti* sonnets, a sequence of eighty-eight poems believed to record his wooing of Elizabeth Boyle, whom he was to marry, or the delightful *Epithalamion* (the meaning, from the Greek, is 'upon the bridechamber') which celebrates his marriage.

Shakespeare to the Romantics

Gavin Ewart, a living poet, has written a witty poem beneath the surface of which a serious point is made:

Xmas for the Boys

A clockwork skating Wordsworth on the ice,
An automatic sermonizing Donne,
A brawling Marlowe shaking out the dice,
A male but metaphysical Thom Gunn.
Get them all now – the latest greatest set
Of all the Poets, dry to sopping wet.

A mad, ferocious, disappointed Swift
Being beaten by a servant in the dark.
Eliot going up to Heaven in a lift,
Shelley going overboard, just for a lark.
Although the tempo and the talent varies
Now is the time to order the whole series.

An electronic Milton, blind as a bat,
A blood-spitting consumptive Keats,
Tennyson calmly raising a tall hat,
Swinburne being whipped in certain dark back
                                    streets.
All working models, correct from head to toe –
But Shakespeare's extra, as you ought to know.

The point Ewart is making here is that the various poets he mentions (as toy models, like literary Action-Men) have all in their different ways been neatly, if falsely, categorised in the public imagination: each is labelled with a biographical characteristic – the young Wordsworth skating on the frozen lake; Donne preaching in St Paul's; Marlowe, who was killed in a tavern brawl, enjoying his punch-up in the local; and so on. Shakespeare, however, is different: we cannot label him or pin him down. Both the private man and his achievement elude definition. He is too various, protean, mysterious: neither his genius nor his personality can be classified.

We are in possession of a few facts about his life. He was born in 1564 at Stratford-on-Avon and educated at the local free grammar school. He married Anne Hathaway in

1582, left Stratford about three years later, and became an actor in the Lord Chamberlain's company of players (known after the accession of James I as the King's Company). He began writing plays in 1590 and seems suddenly to have stopped in 1611 when he returned to Stratford, though in 1613 he acquired a house in Blackfriars. He died in 1616. He wrote over thirty poetic dramas, which include some of the greatest literary works ever created, as well as 154 sonnets and other poems. Had he written the sonnets only he would be a major English poet. What were the circumstances that enabled this breathtaking talent to come to such dazzling fruition?

The first and obvious factor was the state of the English language at the time that Shakespeare was beginning to write. During the couple of centuries since the time of Chaucer it had become the richest, most colourful, vigorous and musical of tongues. It might have lacked the mellifluous softness of Italian or French, but its flavoursome mixture of Latin, French and Anglo-Saxon gave it not only an unusually large vocabulary but a range of sounds and associations missing from more homogeneous languages. Next, and almost equally important, was the fact that, through the labours of his predecessors, from Chaucer to Sidney, he had at his disposal a poetic technique which was capable of serving his imaginative and creative needs. Finally, he was fortunate to have the example of his exact contemporary, Christopher Marlowe, who had written, not later than 1587, his poetic drama in blank verse, *Tamburlaine,* and with whom he almost certainly collaborated on parts of his own earliest plays, *Henry VI* and *Titus Andronicus.*

Marlowe (1564–1593) was the son of a Canterbury shoemaker and educated at King's School, Canterbury and Corpus Christi College, Cambridge. Like Shakespeare he was attached to a company of players, that of the Earl of Nottingham. His best plays, *Edward II* and *Dr Faustus,* contain superb declamatory speeches, and his handling of blank verse shows an ease and assurance which must have encouraged his successors to adopt the measure as the most serviceable metre for poetic drama: it was sufficiently formal to accommodate the most ceremonious use of language, yet readily adapted itself to the rhythms of idiomatic speech.

**Shakespeare
to the
Romantics**

The great flowering of Elizabethan and Jacobean poetic drama produced a literature both exciting and eloquent but which, by its theatrical nature, remained rooted in the common experience of the people it set out to entertain, and employed a language which would be recognised as the tongue of men. The use of poetic dialogue in the theatre, as used by Marlowe, Shakespeare, Ben Jonson, John Webster, Thomas Middleton and others, the necessary relationship between the language spoken by the audience and that by the actors on the stage, confirmed in English poetry the conversational tone which is never entirely absent from even the most formal or lyrical of verse.

John Donne (1572–1631) introduced a new note into English poetry and proved to be the leader of a group of subsequent writers who were called (originally by the poet John Dryden and, later, by Dr Johnson) the Metaphysical School of poets. Among the Metaphysicals were such fine writers as George Herbert, Henry Vaughan and Andrew Marvell, but to modern tastes Donne is probably the most attractive and stimulating. It was he who forged the 'metaphysical' style, a way of fusing passionate feeling with complex thought, and communicating this fusion through the creation of fantastic images which yoked together the most disparate of phenomena, drawing upon, not mythology or past literature, nor careful observation of natural objects, but contemporary technology, mathematics, physics and cartography. To readers of an unscientific cast of mind this might sound most forbidding, but in fact Donne's poetry, both secular and religious, blazes with feeling, sparkles with intelligence, and can often touch a chord of simple tenderness that is the more affecting for its being counterpointed against such brilliant intellectual pyrotechnics.

The name given to the often bizarre metaphors and similes, in which heterogeneous ideas and objects are compared or identified by the Metaphysical poets, is the 'conceit'. To the twentieth-century reader this may seem a puzzling term, but in the seventeenth century the more usual spelling of the word was *conceipt* and its meaning was, and still is – though we tend now to think of it chiefly in the sense of *self-conceit* – something conceived in the mind, a notion or idea, in the case of the Metaphysical poets a fanciful, ingenious and witty expression of a concept. In this well-known poem by Donne we find the joined souls of the two physically separated lovers compared, first to gold, which can be expanded through being beaten, and then, more startlingly, but with ingenious aptness, to a pair of geometrical compasses:

**Shakespeare
to the
Romantics**

A Valediction: Forbidding Mourning

As virtuous men pass mildly away,
And whisper to their souls, to go,
Whilst some of their sad friends do say,
The breath goes now, and some say, no:

So let us melt, and make no noise,
No tear-floods, nor sigh-tempests move,
'Twere profanation of our joys
To tell the laity our love.

Moving of th'earth brings harms and fears,
Men reckon what it did and meant,
But trepidation of the spheres,
Though greater far, is innocent.

Dull sublunary lovers' love
(Whose soul is sense) cannot admit
Absence, because it doth remove
Those things which elemented it.

But we by a love, so much refin'd,
That ourselves know not what it is,
Inter-assurèd of the mind,
Care less eyes, lips, and hands to miss.

Our two souls therefore, which are one,
Though I must go, endure not yet
A breach, but an expansion,
Like gold to aery thinness beat.

If they be two, they are two so
As stiff twin compasses are two,
Thy soul the fixed foot, makes no show
To move, but doth, if th'other do.

And though it in the centre sit,
Yet when the other far doth roam,
It leans, and hearkens after it,
And grows erect, as that comes home.

Such wilt thou be to me, who must
Like th'other foot, obliquely run;
Thy firmness draws my circle just,
And makes me end, where I begun.

Andrew Marvell's celebrated *To His Coy Mistress,* a few lines
of which were quoted in Chapter 3, is a delightfully witty
proposal to his hesitant young lady that she should waste no
time in surrendering to his overtures, and here the poet compares his passion to, of all things, a vegetable, yet contrives to
render this unlikely conjunction of disparate ideas entirely
convincing and charming.

Had we but world enough, and time,
This coyness, Lady, were no crime.
We would sit down and think which way
To walk and pass our long love's day.
Thou by the Indian Ganges' side
Shouldst rubies find: I by the tide
Of Humber would complain. I would
Love you ten years before the Flood,
And you should, if you please, refuse
Till the conversion of the Jews.
My vegetable love should grow
Vaster than empires, and more slow;
An hundred years should go to praise
Thine eyes and on thy forehead gaze;
Two hundred to adore each breast;
But thirty thousand to the rest;
An age at least to every part,
And the last age should show your heart;
For, Lady, you deserve this state,
Nor would I love at lower rate.
    But at my back I always hear
Time's wingèd chariot hurrying near;
And yonder all before us lie
Deserts of vast eternity.
Thy beauty shall no more be found,

Nor, in thy marble vault, shall sound
My echoing song: then worms shall try
That long preserved virginity,
And your quaint honour turn to dust,
And into ashes all my lust:
The grave's a fine and private place,
But none, I think, do there embrace.
    Now therefore, while the youthful hue
Sits on thy skin like morning dew,
And while thy willing soul transpires
At every pore with instant fires,
Now let us sport us while we may,
And now, like amorous birds of prey,
Rather at once our time devour
Than languish in his slow-chapt power.
Let us roll all our strength and all
Our sweetness up into one ball,
And tear our pleasures with rough strife
Thorough the iron gates of life:
Thus, though we cannot make our sun
Stand still, yet we will make him run.

Marvell, born in 1621, became in 1657 assistant to John Milton (1608–1674), who had been appointed Latin secretary to Oliver Cromwell's Council of State but had been afflicted by blindness. Milton's poetry is written almost without exception in the grand style, and the blank verse which he employed for his epic, *Paradise Lost*, is magnificently sonorous but quite incapable of relaxation into lightness of tone. Where the dramatic blank verse of Shakespeare and his contemporaries was flexible and essentially colloquial, *Paradise Lost* is monumental, and the sentence structure is closer to the language of the Latin poets he admired than to the patterns of English speech. A proper appreciation of *Paradise Lost* requires from the reader a considerable knowledge of both the Old Testament and of classical literature, but I believe that some, perhaps many, readers might enjoy the splendour of language and imagery, though I suspect in most cases fairly brief visits to this great cathedral of the poem will be preferable to a prolonged sojourn within its walls.
    Milton's achievement in *Paradise Lost, Samson Agonistes, Comus* and the shorter poems, *Lycidas* and *On the*

Morning of Christ's Nativity, was to produce a poetry in the English language that could stand comparison with the works of classical antiquity; but he had moved as far away as it was possible to travel from plain contemporary speech and his example, splendid as it was, provided a warning to his successors that they must not attempt to emulate or surpass it. His lesser but very gifted and entertaining contemporaries, such as Robert Herrick, Sir John Suckling and Edmund Waller, continued writing in what was essentially the English lyrical vernacular tradition, and the next undeniably major poet, John Dryden (1631–1700), while himself a considerable classicist (he translated the whole of Virgil and parts of Ovid, Homer, Lucretius and Theocritus), determined to embody the classical virtues of formal correctness, lucidity and decorum of language, was also concerned with incorporating the vigorous rhythms and syntax of ordinary speech. Dryden wrote for the theatre in blank verse and in rhymed couplets, which imposed upon him the necessity for immediate comprehensibility and steered him away from the strained artificiality that renders a good deal of the classical or 'Augustan' poetry of the eighteenth century unsympathetic to modern taste.

Dryden's mastery of the heroic couplet provided a model not only for Alexander Pope but for many of the poets of the seventy years or so following Dryden's death. It was not, of course, the only metre used. Jonathan Swift (1667–1745) favoured rhymed octosyllabic couplets which he used with great verve in poems such as *Verses on the Death of Dr Swift* and the sardonic *Phillis, or the Progress of Love;* John Gay (1685–1730), author of *The Beggar's Opera,* wrote in stanzas which anticipated Byron's *Don Juan;* William Collins (1721–1759) wrote complex odes including the fine *Ode to Evening;* and Christopher Smart (1722–1770) employed various verse forms including a kind of liturgical free verse in that fascinating oddity *Jubilate Agno.* Nevertheless the major works of Pope, Goldsmith and Samuel Johnson were written in heroic couplets, and since the eighteenth century the form has never been employed with such confidence and skill.

The lesser poets of the eighteenth century – and here one must include authors of great accomplishment, such as Thomas Gray, who could not quite equal Pope for brilliance of wit, invention and the sense of verbal propriety, sometimes found themselves trapped by the strict formality of technique into using speech patterns that bore no relation whatsoever to the language spoken in the street. A special syntax and vocabulary came to be used and, as the century wore on, this stylised 'poetic diction' became more and more stilted and artificial, so far removed from the language of good prose or good talk that it seemed impossible for the bards of the time to make a direct statement on even the simplest subject.

When Gray, in *On a Distant Prospect of Eton College*, writes:

> Say, Father Thames, for thou hast seen
> Full many a sprightly race
> Disporting on thy margent green
> The paths of pleasure trace,
> Who foremost now delight to cleave
> With pliant arm thy glassy wave?
> The captive linnet which enthrall?
> What idle progeny succeed
> To chase the rolling circle's speed,
> Or urge the flying ball?

the twentieth-century reader will be instantly struck by the almost comical convolutions of the language. The fifth and sixth lines have a certain charm, but Gray does seem to be straining rather hard to avoid saying, 'who now enjoys swimming in you the most?', and the last three lines make heavy weather of 'What children are now bowling hoops or kicking a ball?' When the reader has made the necessary imaginative transference back to the time in which Gray's poem was written the lines can give some pleasure, but the manner, when adopted by a lesser poet, becomes merely irritating or absurd.

William Blake (1757–1827), who was self-educated, was remarkably unaffected by the poetic fashions of his youth, and his private vision of reality was so powerful that it demanded a style of greater austerity and directness for its expression. He is unquestionably a great poet, as these few lines will show:

London

I wander thro' each charter'd street,
Near where the charter'd Thames does flow,
And mark in every face I meet
Marks of weakness, marks of woe.

In every cry of every Man,
In every Infant's cry of fear,
In every voice, in every ban,
The mind-forg'd manacles I hear.

How the Chimney-sweeper's cry
Every black'ning Church appalls;
And the hapless Soldier's sigh
Runs in blood down Palace walls.

But most thro' midnight streets I hear
How the youthful Harlot's curse
Blasts the new born Infant's tear,
And blights with plagues the Marriage hearse.

But, especially in his long prophetic works, in which he creates a private mythology of good and evil, he is so individualistic in both content and style that his breakaway from current modes of composition could offer little in the way of guidance to young poets, who were inclined to rebel against the stagnating formality and ossified poetic diction of the later and lesser Augustans. It was left to William Wordsworth (1770–1850) and Samuel Taylor Coleridge (1772–1834) to lead the movement in English poetry that has been designated 'Romantic', as opposed to the 'Classical' spirit of the eighteenth century. However a good case could be made out for naming Blake as the first of the great Romantics, for it was Blake who repeatedly denounced in his poems the omnipotence of human reason, which had been enthroned by the Augustans, and who asserted the supremacy of imagination and instinct as guides to ultimate truth.

Wordworth's rebellion against the beliefs and practices of the eighteenth-century poets took a dual form: first, reflecting the spirit of his own times, he rejected reason as the

God-like quality in man and asserted the divine power of the imagination. The romantic hero figure was no longer the great warrior or ruler, but the individual whose explorations were directed into his own consciousness. *The Prelude,* the finest and most ambitious long poem of the period, did not deal with deeds of heroism performed by the man of action, as did the classical epics, nor with the drama of Man's Fall, through choosing evil in preference to good, as did Milton's *Paradise Lost;* it did not attack the Goddess of Dullness who posed a threat to established social order and reason, as did Pope's *Dunciad. The Prelude,* as its sub-title, *The Growth of the Poet's Mind,* states, is an exploration of the author's own responses to experience: the hero is the poet himself.

Next, Wordsworth rebelled against the language of eighteenth-century poetry, that special circumlocutory, latinate vocabulary and syntax, and asserted, in his preface to the second edition of the *Lyrical Ballads,* that:

> My purpose was to imitate and as far as possible to adopt the very language of men . . . There will be found in these volumes little of what is usually called poetic diction, as much pains has been taken to avoid it as is usually taken to produce it . . . It may be safely affirmed that there neither is, nor can be, any *essential* difference between the language of prose and metrical composition.

In principle these views acted as a salutary corrective to the over-decorated and long-winded locutions of the worst of the minor Augustans, though in practice a too rigid adherence to them resulted in some banal and even absurd verses. At his very considerable best, in such poems as *The Prelude, Tintern Abbey, Resolution and Independence,* many of the sonnets and the *Immortality Ode,* Wordsworth wisely forgets his own proscriptions and allows himself to make use of the whole range of available language, modulating from the most simple and direct words and syntax to a rich, complex and rhetorical splendour. Here are the first two stanzas of *Resolution and Independence:*

There was a roaring in the wind all night;
The rain came heavily and fell in floods;
But now the sun is rising calm and bright;
The birds are singing in the distant woods;
Over his own sweet voice the Stock-dove broods;
The Jay makes answer as the Magpie chatters;
And all the air is filled with pleasant noise of waters.

All things that love the sun are out of doors;
The sky rejoices in the morning's birth;
The grass is bright with rain-drops; – on the moors
The hare is running races in her mirth;
And with her feet she from the plashy earth
Raises a mist, that, glittering in the sun,
Runs with her all the way, wherever she doth run.

The poem proceeds cheerfully enough for another four stanzas, but suddenly an irrational fit of melancholy, despite the glorious weather and scenery, descends on the poet, and he starts to contemplate the possible terrors and privations that the future may hold for him, and he broods upon the fate of the poets, Chatterton and Burns, both of whom died young and in misery, the seventeen-year-old Chatterton by his own hand:

I thought of Chatterton, the marvellous Boy,
The sleepless Soul that perished in his pride;
Of him who walked in glory and in joy
 Following his plough, along the mountain-side:
By our own spirits are we deified:
We Poets in our youth begin in gladness;
But thereof come in the end despondency and
                              madness.

Here, both language and syntax are more formal than in the previous stanzas, and Wordsworth does not hesitate to employ a more resonant vocabulary and verbal music appropriate to his more highly charged subject matter.

The Romantic movement of the earlier part of the nineteenth century, with its emphasis on a return to the rhythms and vocabulary of common speech and its preoccupation with the primary importance of the individual consciousness and imagination, its insistence on the value of passionate feeling over cool reason, found its perfect representative in John Keats (1795–1821) whose *Ode to a Nightingale* must surely stand as the archetypal Romantic lyric in our language. Keats is here affirming the primacy of emotion over reason, and the structure of the poem is dependent on impulse and association; there is none of the rational sequentiality that an Augustan ode would display. The *Ode to a Nightingale* begins with a direct statement of personal feeling, 'My heart aches. . .', and at least a partial longing for death. Then the song of the nightingale is introduced, followed by subjective images evoked by the music. Gradually we realise that the nightingale is serving at one moment as an emblem of unconscious, instinctive life, in contrast to the poet's awareness of self and his own mortality; at other times the bird's song and the poet's own song become one, so that the nightingale becomes a symbol of lyric poetry or perhaps of the capriciousness of poetic inspiration.

Ode to a Nightingale

My heart aches, and a drowsy numbness pains
My sense, as though of hemlock I had drunk,
Or emptied some dull opiate to the drains
One minute past, and Lethe-wards had sunk:
'Tis not through envy of thy happy lot,
But being too happy in thy happiness, –
That thou, light-wingèd Dryad of the trees,
In some melodious plot
Of beechen green, and shadows numberless,
Singest of summer in full-throated ease.

O, for a draught of vintage! that hath been
Cooled a long age in the deep-delvèd earth,
Tasting of Flora and the country green,
Dance, and Provençal song, and sunburnt mirth:
O for a beaker full of the warm South,
Full of the true, the blushful Hippocrene,
With beaded bubbles winking at the brim,
And purple-stainèd mouth;
That I might drink, and leave the world unseen,
And with thee fade away into the forest dim:

Fade far away, dissolve, and quite forget
What thou among the leaves hast never known,
The weariness, the fever, and the fret
Here, where men sit and hear each other groan;
Where palsy shakes a few, sad, last grey hairs,
Where youth grows pale, and spectre-thin, and dies;
Where but to think is to be full of sorrow
And leaden-eyed despairs,
Where Beauty cannot keep her lustrous eyes,
Or new Love pine at them beyond to-morrow.

Away! away! for I will fly to thee,
Not charioted by Bacchus and his pards,
But on the viewless wings of Poesy,
Though the dull brain perplexes and retards:
Already with thee! tender is the night,
And haply the Queen-Moon is on her throne,
Cluster'd around by all her starry Fays;
But here there is no light,
Save what from heaven is with the breezes blown
Through verdurous glooms and winding mossy ways.

I cannot see what flowers are at my feet,
Nor what soft incense hangs upon the boughs,
But, in embalmèd darkness, guess each sweet
Wherewith the seasonable month endows
The grass, the thicket, and the fruit-tree wild;
White hawthorn, and the pastoral eglantine;
Fast fading violets cover'd up in leaves;
And mid-May's eldest child,
The coming musk-rose, full of dewy wine,
The murmurous haunt of flies on summer eves.

Darkling I listen; and, for many a time
I have been half in love with easeful Death,
Call'd him soft names in many a musèd rhyme,
To take into the air my quiet breath;
Now more than ever seems it rich to die,
To cease upon the midnight with no pain,
While thou art pouring forth thy soul abroad
In such an ecstasy!
Still wouldst thou sing, and I have ears in vain –
To thy high requiem become a sod.

Thou wast not born for death, immortal Bird!
No hungry generations tread thee down;
The voice I hear this passing night was heard
In ancient days by emperor and clown:
Perhaps the self-same song that found a path
Through the sad heart of Ruth, when, sick for home,
She stood in tears amid the alien corn;
The same that oft-times hath
Charm'd magic casements, opening on the foam
Of perilous seas, in faery lands forlorn.

Forlorn: the very word is like a bell
To toll me back from thee to my sole self!
Adieu! the fancy cannot cheat so well
As she is fam'd to do, deceiving elf.
Adieu! adieu! thy plaintive anthem fades
Past the near meadows, over the still stream,
Up the hillside; and now 'tis buried deep
In the next valley-glades:
Was it a vision, or a waking dream?
Fled is that music: – Do I wake or sleep?

The deaths of Coleridge, Keats, Shelley and Byron, all of which took place before Queen Victoria came to the throne, closed a poetic era, that of early nineteenth-century Romanticism, and made way for the entry of the Victorians, but the Romantic spirit was still very much alive and may be seen in various forms in the work of the major Victorian poets and continuing into the present century.

the Victorians to 1960

The two giants of Victorian English poetry are Tennyson (1809–1892) and Browning (1812–1889), though I believe a strong case could be made out for including Matthew Arnold (1822–1888) in their august company. There are two other fine poets of great importance but neither of these, for different reasons, can be easily categorised as Victorian, although both lived and wrote during her reign. Gerard Manley Hopkins

(1844–1889), educated at Highgate School and Balliol College, Oxford, was converted to Roman Catholicism in 1866
and entered the Jesuit novitiate in 1868. His poems, which
were formally remarkably original – too original for the time
when they were written – did not receive proper publication
until 1918 when Robert Bridges edited them. These poems
have exercised a profound influence on many twentieth-
century poets of reputation, including W. H. Auden, Dylan
Thomas and the living poet Ted Hughes, and though Hopkins
died during Queen Victoria's reign, his literary place seems to
have established itself among the innovatory moderns.

Thomas Hardy (1840–1928), as poet rather than novelist, appears to belong more naturally in the twentieth century,
rather than in the nineteenth. This is partly because his first
volume of poetry was not published until the very end of Victoria's reign, and, after the appearance of his novel *Jude the
Obscure* in 1896, he wrote nothing but poetry, and partly, more
important perhaps, because his true poetic greatness has not
been fully recognised until quite recently.

Tennyson, who was appointed Poet Laureate in succession to Wordsworth in 1850, is the very archetype of the
late Romantic poet. His skill and versatility as a craftsman of
verse are unsurpassed: he possessed a magical lyric gift (see
Now Sleeps the Crimson Petal in the previous chapter), and
much of his work is tinged with a sweet, melodious melancholy that is deeply characteristic of the period. These few
lines of blank verse from *Tithonus* will demonstrate his gift for
the haunting cadence and image:

> The woods decay, the woods decay and fall,
> The vapours weep their burthen to the ground,
> Man comes and tills the field and lies beneath,
> And after many a summer dies the swan.
> Me only cruel immortality
> Consumes: I wither slowly in thine arms,
> Here at the quiet limit of the world,
> A white-hair'd shadow roaming like a dream
> The ever-silent spaces of the East,
> Far-folded mists, and gleaming halls of morn.

Robert Browning is a poet of a very different kind, both stylis-
tically and temperamentally. He too possessed a strong lyric

gift, but the rhythms and language of his lyrical verse are less
autumnal than those of Tennyson, and he is more concerned
than his great contemporary with basing the cadences and
syntax of his lines on those of the plain speaking voice. His
most influential and pleasing innovation was his use of the
dramatic monologue, where the poet adopts the persona (or
dramatic mask) of an invented or historical figure. In the poem
Confessions we find the conversational tone combined with
the lyric, as an old man on his deathbed, attended by a priest,
reflects aloud on his past amorous adventures:

What is he buzzing in my ears?
'Now that I come to die,
Do I view the world as a vale of tears?'
Ah, reverend sir, not I:

What I viewed there once, what I view again
Where the physic bottles stand
On the table's edge, – is a suburb lane,
With a wall to my bedside hand.

That land sloped, much as the bottles do,
From a house you could descry
O'er the garden-wall: is the curtain blue
Or green to a healthy eye?

To mine, it serves for the old June weather
Blue above lane and wall;
And that farthest bottle labelled 'Ether'
Is the house o'ertopping all.

At a terrace, somewhere near the stopper,
There watched for me, one June,
A girl: I know, sir, it's improper,
My poor mind's out of tune.

Only, there was a way . . . you crept
Close by the side, to dodge
Eyes in the house, two eyes except:
They styled their house 'The Lodge.'

What right had a lounger up their lane?
But, by creeping very close,
With the good wall's help, – their eyes might strain
And stretch themselves to Oes,

Yet never catch her and me together,
As she left the attic, there,
By the rim of the bottle labelled 'Ether',
And stole from stair to stair,

And stood by the rose-wreathed gate. Alas,
We loved, sir – used to meet:
How sad and bad and mad it was –
But then, how it was sweet!

It was in the early nineteenth century that American poets began to discover their own identity and produce poetry that, though closely related to the work of British writers in diction and form, contained elements that were specifically of the New World. Both Ralph Waldo Emerson (1803–1882) and Henry David Thoreau (1817–1862) wrote rugged, honest verse which showed a different attitude to nature from that of European poets, an attitude which reflected the struggle of the settler in a hostile natural environment which must be subdued before the task of establishing a civilised society could be accomplished. Already we can perceive a resistance to orthodox metres in the harsher and irregular rhythms of their verses, an independence that was to assert itself powerfully in the free verse of Walt Whitman.

Henry Wadsworth Longfellow (1807–1882) did not display in his work a similar independence and sense of national identity, for he was both highly educated (he became Professor of Modern Languages at Harvard) and widely travelled in Europe, and Herman Melville (1819–1891), the author of the great novel *Moby Dick*, though emphatically nationalistic in his literary aims, did not quite manage to incorporate into his often vivid poems the patterns of American colloquial speech, but remained largely dependent on British models.

Perhaps surprisingly, after Whitman, the first major poetic American voice with a totally distinctive accent was that of a Massachusetts spinster who spent her whole life in almost total seclusion, and published – though without her own consent – only two poems while she was alive. Emily Dickinson (1830–1886) was a writer of indisputable genius whose short, gnomic utterances on love and mortality are among the most disturbing and original of nineteenth-century poetry in the English language. Here is a typical Dickinson poem which presents striking visual images of a snake, and uncannily conveys its power, as both symbol and living creature, to evoke feelings of dread:

> A narrow fellow in the grass
> Occasionally rides;
> You may have met him, – did you not?
> His notice sudden is.
>
> The grass divides as with a comb,
> A spotted shaft is seen;
> And then it closes at your feet
> And opens further on.
>
> He likes a boggy acre,
> A floor too cool for corn.
> Yet when a child, and barefoot,
> I more than once, at morn,
>
> Have passed, I thought, a whip-lash
> Unbraiding in the sun, –
> When, stooping to secure it,
> It wrinkled, and was gone.
>
> Several of nature's people
> I know, and they know me;
> I feel for them a transport
> Of cordiality;
>
> But never met this fellow,
> Attended or alone,
> Without a tighter breathing,
> And zero at the bone.

From the end of the nineteenth century to the present, American and English poetry has moved together in a not always easy relationship, the achievements and preoccupations of one country sometimes dominating, and at others being dominated by, those of the other. In the early twentieth century, after the langours and longueurs of the late Victorians such as Swinburne and the less accomplished Francis Thompson, Lionel Johnson and Ernest Dowson, English poets strove, by attempting a more robust kind of realism, either to absorb the life of modern cities into the imagery of their work, or to attempt a refurbishing of the tradition of pastoral or nature poetry. Until quite recently it has been fashionable to dismiss much of the verse written in the decade or so before the outbreak of the First World War, but, as is now more generally recognised, excellent and moving poems were produced by writers like A. E. Housman, Rudyard Kipling, Walter de la Mare and John Masefield. One towering figure, however, emerged at that time, the Irish poet W. B. Yeats (1865–1939), who in his youth wrote exquisite romantic verse, incorporating a dream-like mythology based on Irish folklore, but who steadily developed and refined his gift until, in the 1920s and 1930s, he was creating magnificent poetry mythologising the country and people of Ireland and probing deeply into the permanent questions of man's relation to the world he lives in, the nature of love, government and art.

The First World War, of course, inflicted deep and long-lasting wounds on the consciousness of European and, to a lesser extent, American man, but in meeting the challenge presented by the experience of modern warfare English poetry was to some degree revitalised. The poets of the First World War were not only recording and exploring their personal confrontations with battle in a subjective way, they were also acting as self-appointed recorders of the truth. The propaganda disseminated by the press and politicians was intent on concealing the appalling realities of war: language was used to glorify the abominable, hoodwink the gullible, and allay the fears of the timid. The poets' task, apart from the primary one of making poetry out of such nightmarish material, was to report to those at home, who had been so grossly misled, the true nature of Armageddon; they felt compelled to turn away from the trivial and self-indulgent preoccupations that had provided the subject matter of much Edwardian and early Georgian verse, and find ways of communicating the results of their exploration of the hell that was modern warfare.

Wilfred Owen, who was killed just before the Armistice in 1918, aged only twenty-six, rapidly developed from a youthful poetaster, playing with decorative romantic imagery and diction, to a poet who created a searing representation of sacrifice, waste and suffering. Siegfried Sassoon, a few years older than Owen, changed from a minor lyricist, celebrating country pleasures, to a savage satirist and stern recorder of the horrors he experienced on the Western Front. Isaac Rosenberg, killed in 1918, a painter as well as a poet, produced verbal pictures of trench warfare that have haunted the imagination of succeeding generations. The war poetry of these writers and others, like Edmund Blunden, Robert Graves and David Jones, also a distinguished painter, presented subsequent poets with a way of writing that would prove serviceable when in the bitter social and political climate of the 1920s and 1930s they came to deal with the brave new world which they had inherited. But this style, one of direct and precisely observed realism, was not the only one that the new generation of poets employed.

What is known, in the literary history of the twentieth century, as the Modern Movement began in the years of the First World War and came to its zenith with the first, possibly the only, major work engendered by it, T. S. Eliot's *The Waste Land*. Eliot (1888–1965) was born at St Louis, Missouri, but he became a British subject in 1927. His friend and colleague Ezra Pound was born in Idaho in 1885, though despite spending much of his adult life in England, Paris and Italy, he retained his American citizenship.

The Modern Movement began in the second decade of the twentieth century with a group of poets, British and American, who called themselves the Imagists. Their aim was to write short poems in free rhythms, avoiding orthodox metre and rhyme, and concentrating on producing sharply observed, concrete images, offering nothing in the way of generalisation or comment. Here is an example by the English Imagist, T. E. Hulme, who was killed in the First World War:

Autumn

A touch of cold in the Autumn night –
I walked abroad,
And saw the ruddy moon lean over a hedge
Like a red-faced farmer.
I did not stop to speak, but nodded,
And round about were wistful stars
With white faces like town children.

As the reader will see from this quite highly regarded example the effect can be very pleasing, but the limitations in terms of both content and form are much too restrictive to enable anything of great value to be produced beyond neat verbal miniatures. Nevertheless, it was from the notion of freeing the poet from the conventions of traditional prosody and producing images rather than exposition and discourse that modernism began. However, as we find from a reading of *The Waste Land*, published in 1922, the new poetry became capable of far more than mere presentation of vivid word pictures, though the 'meaning' of this poem in the prose, paraphrasable sense, remains ambiguous and elusive, but not impenetrably so.

The Waste Land is a poem which, while conforming to the modernists' demand that traditional prescribed metre should be eschewed, nevertheless takes the iambic pentameter of blank verse as its base and plays variations upon this measure; it is not, in the strict sense, free verse but verse which moves fairly freely on a strong leash of metrical regularity.

My advice to any reader coming to *The Waste Land* for the first time is not to worry about grasping the 'meaning' in the sense in which a conventional narrative has meaning. A single perusal of the poem will at least convey the author's sense of disillusionment with modern (i.e. post-First World War) metropolitan life, though it is a romantic disillusionment, and one which is threaded, one feels, on a kind of melancholy relish. Images of twentieth-century London are juxtaposed against images—which sometimes take the form of quotations from Spenser and other poets of the past – of the city of Elizabeth I's reign. The poem, in fact, proceeds through counterpointed images and contains no clear sequential or narrative line. It may not be an accident that it should have been written when the art of the cinema was becoming worth serious attention, and it employs a technique of strong visual images, cuts, dissolves and flashbacks that could be described as cinematic.

Of course there is far more to *The Waste Land* than I have suggested here: there are parallels with, and oblique references to, pagan rituals and myth; it is clear that Eliot's city is not only the historical and geographical capital but a symbolic place, an urban wilderness where spiritual values have perished or are perishing. Frequent re-readings of the poem – and it is one one that yields greater pleasure on each return to it – and a readiness to allow the images and rhythms to do their own work on the ear and imagination will remove the barriers that some critics of the poem have themselves erected through approaching it in the wrong way, asking it to offer them a rational, paraphrasable 'message' which it was no part of the poet's intention to convey.

While the American poets, Eliot and Pound, were, in a relatively small way, changing the course of English poetry, home-based US poets were busily and firmly establishing a national tradition of poetry which was distinctively their own and not a transatlantic echo of English styles and forms. Robert Frost (1875–1963), whose splendid poems are all written in traditional English forms, nevertheless speaks with an unmistakably American voice. William Carlos Williams (1883–1963), who has proved to be one of the most influential upon his fellow countrymen of the poets of the twentieth century, experimented with forms which rejected the stressed metres of orthodox English verse, and aimed at a more natural, colloquial rhythm, which would more easily accommodate the cadences and idioms of American speech than the formal measures of English prosody.

At the risk of over-simplifying, twentieth-century American poetry may be divided into two kinds; the formal traditional verse, the distinctively American quality of which is recognised by the local imagery and references and a subtle adaptation of indigenous speech rhythms to the familiar movement of English metrics, and the much freer colloquial verse, originally inspired by Whitman, and refined and developed by Williams, Pound and their followers. Of one thing there can be no question: American poetry today is no longer dependent on European models. It grows strongly from its own soil and it is the British poet who is more likely to be influenced by, rather than influence, his transatlantic counterpart.

The Modern Movement in a small way changed the course of poetry in Britain by causing its followers to be more exploratory in their use of rhythms, to be prepared to experiment in verbal patterns based on principles other than those of traditional stress metre, to aim at employing a diction that is at once precise, evocative and conversational, and to communicate states of feeling through images rather than discourse. But *The Waste Land* itself did not serve as a model for younger poets. It is a unique, perhaps great, literary work, but it is not one that could point towards a direction in which succeeding writers might find a way of shaping their own vision of the world. In fact the best younger poets of the 1930s, while profiting from Eliot's example in the matter of the fastidious selection of exact language and persuasive imagery, and the skilful versifying of contemporary natural speech, deliberately turned away from attempts to create a great panoramic myth of a culture in decay, and concentrated either on the pains and delights of personal relationships or on more immediate social and political problems.

W. H. Auden (1907–1973) was the leading young poet of the 1930s and, while profiting from Eliot's earlier and more traditional verse, and from his exemplary diction, he turned back to the varied but always regularly metrical verse of Thomas Hardy for the structuring of his poems. Hardy, of course, was by no means his only influence. Auden was immensely versatile, both in his use of orthodox poetic forms and in breadth of subject matter and style, writing sonnets, ballads, songs, terza rima, long narratives in Byronic stanzas, Anglo-Saxon alliterative metre, verse plays, opera libretti and verse commentaries for documentary films. Just to give a brief example of his skill in choosing precisely the right metre for his subject, here are a few lines from his commentary for a GPO film in which the reader will hear the insistent, regular beat of the train's wheels on the track:

Night Mail

This is the Night Mail crossing the Border,
Bringing the cheque and the postal order,

Letters for the rich, letters for the poor,
The shop at the corner, the girl next door,

Pulling up Beattock, a steady climb:
The gradient's against her, but she's on time.

Past cotton-grass and moorland boulder,
Shovelling white steam over her shoulder,

Snorting noisily, she passes
Silent miles of wind-bent grasses.

Birds turn their heads as she approaches,
Stare from bushes at her blank-faced coaches.

Sheep-dogs cannot turn her course;
They slumber on with paws across.

In the farm she passes no one wakes,
But a jug in a bedroom gently shakes.

Auden's style, its liveliness and directness, its remarkable capability for dealing with all manner of contemporary experience, from the lyrical subjective to large public events, served as a valuable model for some of the best poets who wrote directly about their experiences in the armed forces in the Second World War. Among them were Roy Fuller and Charles Causley, who wrote some excellent poems about their service in the Royal Navy, and Alun Lewis and Keith Douglas, both of whom lost their lives while serving in the Army. Oddly, very little poetry of any interest was produced by serving members of the RAF.

The poetry of Auden, and his friend Louis MacNeice (1907–1963), was not, however, the only verse style of the 1930s and 1940s. One group of poets in the 1940s exhibited a violent reaction against the control, lucidity and intelligence of Audenesque verse, which was viewed as lacking the visionary and magical incantatory qualities which should inform true poetry. This was a manifestation of the old conflict between the Romantic and Classical views of literature, though these Neo-Romantics, who called themselves the New Apocalypse, would not have received much sympathy from the Romantic poets of the nineteenth century, who would have been totally bewildered by their often incoherent outpourings.

The Apocalypse poets, who included such little-known authors as Henry Treece, J. F. Hendry and Dorian Cooke, claimed the brilliant young Welsh author, Dylan Thomas, as their leader, but in fact none of his best work was remotely related to that of his self-styled followers. Thomas's first collection, *18 Poems*, published when he was only twenty, was one of the most impressive literary debuts of the century, and his great lyric and visionary gifts have assured him a permanent place in the history of English poetry. Although one might detect the influence of Gerard Manley Hopkins in the sweep and surge of his rhythms and the coruscation of consonants and vowels, his work is curiously individual, and attempts by his admirers on both sides of the Atlantic to imitate his style were unfailingly disastrous. Yet there were many poets who did try to echo his splendid incantatory manner, and it was against these Neo-Romantics, and their naive belief in the poetic effectiveness of spontaneous, undisciplined rant, that a group of English poets in the 1950s deliberately set out to re-establish the literary virtues of intelligence, order, common sense, craftsmanship and a respect for traditional verse forms. This group was known simply as the Movement, and it produced at least one fine poet, Philip Larkin (b 1922), whose first important collection (he had published a book of very promising juvenilia in 1945) was *The Less Deceived,* published in 1955, which received universal and well-merited critical acclaim.

I am well aware that this chapter is a blinkered and breathless scramble through the centuries, and that a vast number of fine poets and a huge quantity of great poetry have been entirely ignored, but I hope that it has done a little towards showing that there is always, in whatever era, a constant relationship between the spoken language and the language of poetry, and that this relationship may be, at one time, one of intimacy, when each draws very close to the other, and at other times a distancing when the language of poetry feels the need to assert its right to become an ideal utterance, withdrawing from the patterns and sounds of demotic speech, a sublimation of the intercourse of the marketplace and drawing-room. In English poetry, from the fourteenth century to the mid-twentieth, we hear over and over again the tongues of men and of angels, and sometimes a fusion of the two. What the reader of the poetry being written today, or in the past decade or so, is likely to hear will be discussed in the following chapter.

7

POETRY
NOW

At any given time in history the literary scene will seem confused to those who are living through it, and it is the selectivity of posterity that makes the pattern and orders of eminence appear clearly defined to the retrospective view. Nevertheless it is fairly safe to say that, at the present time, there is an especially bewildering complex of poetic tendencies, kinds of poetry being written, warring factions, ways of presenting, criticising and teaching poetry, and conflicting beliefs about the rôle of the poet in society.

Very broadly speaking there are two principal dualities in contemporary poetry: first, the oppositions between the advocates of unstructured free forms and the devotees of carefully structured verse, whose techniques are based upon traditional practices; and, second, the reciprocal mistrust and disapproval shown by the seriously committed 'literary' writers, whose poems are intended to be printed and read on the page, and the 'popular', performing poets who, while they will probably publish their verses in magazines and collections, are happier declaiming them to an audience. Of course these divisions are far from absolute. Many serious poets, who com-

pose primarily for the printed page, are also perfectly prepared to read their work aloud at public gatherings, and some
of the so-called 'pop' poets clearly cherish serious literary
ambitions and, indeed, are taken seriously by some critics and
teachers of literature.

The practice of promoting public poetry readings has
been steadily increasing over the past twenty years or so, and
these functions now seem to be a stable part of British cultural
life. The readings take many forms. Small literary societies in
provincial towns conduct them in church halls or the sitting-
rooms of their members; schools and colleges invite poets to
read and talk to audiences of students; arts festivals often
advertise poetry readings by well-known authors on their
programmes; international poetry festivals have been held in
London at the Queen Elizabeth Hall and the Albert Hall; less
ambitious events have taken place at the Poetry Society's
headquarters, the Institute of Contemporary Arts, public libraries, public houses and countless other venues in London
and other large cities. An organisation called the National
Poetry Secretariat subsidises public readings all over the
country, and regional arts associations give financial support
to those held in their area. The consequences of all these
events, and of poets being more or less obliged to become
public performers, are manifold and of uncertain benefit to
them as artists.

For the 'pop' poets, whose work has been composed
expressly for the purpose of recital to live audiences, the issue
is plain: writers such as the entertaining Liverpool comic
turns, Adrian Henri and Roger McGough, can only profit from
public performance. Their verses are very simple in both form
and content, and can be assimilated at a single hearing; it is
on the printed page that the deficiencies of thought, technique
and imagination become clear. The poet who is dedicated to
his craft, and is doing his best to continue and develop what is
finest in the tradition of English poetry, which involves com-
pressing the maximum amount of passion, thought, wit and
vision into the smallest possible space and achieving rhythmic
effects of great variety and subtlety, is unlikely to be appreciated by an audience which is probably encountering his
work for the first time. The danger here is, not that he will

be tempted to emulate the content and style of the enter-
tainers, but that he might, in the effort to achieve instant
communication, read only his most readily accessible work
which is quite likely to be his slightest and least characteristic.

Attendance at poetry readings cannot be a substitute
for reading poetry on the page, though it can be an enjoyable
and instructive adjunct. To hear a good poet read his work
aloud, even if he is not an accomplished public speaker, is a
valuable guide as to where the precise emphases are to be
placed, but it is desirable that the audience should either follow the reading with the text before them or have a prior
knowledge of the poems being spoken. The principal justification for popular recitals of poetry, where the readings are
sometimes interspersed with musical items (jazz and poetry
used to be a very popular mixture), is that audiences will come
to associate poetry with pleasure and not feel that it is an
art available only to an initiated minority.

A large number of recordings of poetry have been
made, some featuring speakers, often well-known actors,
reading great poems of the past, and others offering the voice
of the poet himself reading his own work. BBC Radio regularly
broadcasts poetry programmes, again with the actors or the
poets themselves delivering the lines, though a disprop-
ortionately small amount of time is devoted to the art compared with music, drama, documentary programmes and light
entertainment. Television, though it has made a few half-
hearted attempts at broadcasting poetry, has never succeeded
in finding a satisfactory format for its presentation. The trouble is that the projection of concrete visual images on to the
screen, which television producers seem to find irresistible,
only distracts from the words, weakening their impact and
diluting or obfuscating the images that they would engender
in the listener's (or viewer's) mind. Perhaps the only way to do
it successfully – and I am sure this would not appeal to any
television producer – would be to have the poet or reader
speaking the lines while they were displayed on the screen.
Dull stuff? Well, that would depend entirely on the quality of
the words.

One of the most difficult problems faced by someone
coming to English poetry for the first time is not only the

variety of its forms and aims, but the bewildering differences in opinion as to what in fact constitutes a poem. Much of what I read in magazines, anthologies and collections of British and American poetry not only fails to engage my sympathies or give me pleasure, but causes positive irritation and boredom. With some poets in the 1960s and 1970s the traditional Romantic preoccupation with self as hero has degenerated from the Wordsworthian concern with the individual as a representative of mankind to an obsessive infatuation with the poet's private world, with his or her exclusively personal neuroses, anxieties and desires. The poems written by many of these 'confessional' poets seem to proceed, not from a wish to isolate and explore those human qualities, aspirations, fears and hopes that are shared with the rest of mankind, but from a lunatic conviction that, because they themselves are unique individuals, anything they write about themselves is uniquely interesting.

It is, I believe, a healthy sign that the most promising of the younger poets writing at the present time are deeply concerned with the craft of poetry; we can see from their methods of composition that they know that the making of a poem is not a self-indulgent outpouring of disorganised feeling but an art as demanding as any other art form. Tony Harrison has reintroduced the rhymed couplet into modern verse and he employs it with admirable skill and panache. His work in the theatre has probably helped him here, for he has translated with great success, Molière's verse play *Le Misanthrope*, and Racine's *Phèdre*, for National Theatre productions. John Fuller, the son of the former Professor of Poetry at Oxford, Roy Fuller, is a most resourceful writer who has made use of a wide range of traditional metres and stanza forms, and Seamus Heaney, widely recognised as the leading poet of his generation, is a thoughtful master of the craft of verse.

Poetry today occupies a curious place in our cultural and social life, and attitudes towards it have changed considerably in the years following the end of the Second World War. Nowhere can the changes be seen more clearly than in the way in which it is taught in our schools. Older readers will no doubt remember studying the works of Chaucer, Shakespeare, Milton and perhaps those eighteenth- and nineteenth-century poets found in Palgrave's *Golden Treasury* – Thomas Gray, Wordsworth and Tennyson – but virtually no reference would have been made to living writers. Now the case is dramatically altered. Not only living poets, but quite young ones, are studied in our schools, and their writings are set for examinations. Under the auspices of local arts associations' 'Writers in Schools' scheme, poets are quite frequently invited to go into the classroom and read and discuss their poems with students of all ages and levels of ability. In some cases schools and colleges will offer hospitality to a 'resident poet' who will spend a term or longer working with students, discussing literature, conducting poetry 'workshops' and doing his best to encourage original work. Courses in 'creative writing' or simply in poetry writing, which usually last for a working week, are organised by local education authorities or by such organisations as the Arvon Foundation, which offers sessions at two centres, one in Devon and the other in Yorkshire, details of which should be obtainable from any public library. On the face of it contemporary poetry is a flourishing art; any publisher or editor of a magazine which prints verse, or anyone who has been involved as an adjudicator in a poetry competition, will know that thousands of people are busily trying to write poetry. So what precisely is the status and function of the poet in society today?

There are many people, young and old, male and female, who describe themselves as poets, either because they have actually written a few lines of verse, and even in some cases published them, or because they have adopted what they believe to be the manner and manners of the poet, an eccentric non-conformity of dress and behaviour, though it is unlikely that these people have written or even read much, or any, genuine poetry. One can often detect in the collective attitude of the unliterary to the poet a mixture of contempt, perhaps of fear and a kind of superstitious awe, and their prejudices are usually buttressed, not by a knowledge of real poets and poetry, but by caricatures of the charlatan and self-deluded exhibitionist.

The true poet in the last twenty-five years, or for that matter at any other time, is likely to be someone quite different from the vulgar image. He is almost certain to follow some other profession, writing in his spare time, and that profession is likely to be a socially responsible one: many living poets are full- or part-time teachers in schools, colleges or universities; at least three are doctors; others are solicitors, BBC producers, journalists, nurses and clergymen, to mention only a few occupations followed by established poets. Official recognition of the poet's importance, however, is not generously bestowed.

The office of Poet Laureate, which was first officially conferred on John Dryden by Charles II, originally meant that the recipient of the honour became an officer of the Royal Household; his duties involved the writing of suitable odes for state occasions, royal events and national triumphs, for which he received a small stipend. Today it is little more than a token form of recognition, though Laureates of the twentieth century, including the present one, Sir John Betjeman, have written a few verses celebrating such royal events as a marriage or birth of a child. The Laureateship has been held by some fine poets, such as Wordsworth and Tennyson, but it has also been conferred upon a number of minor and even distinctly feeble authors like Alfred Austin, who succeeded Tennyson and wrote a poem on the Jameson Raid which contained this preposterous couplet:

> They rode across the veldt
> As fast as they could pelt.

But the poet is unlikely to receive much in the way of public honours because his art is not a suitable medium for the celebration of large events, especially at the present time when prose and the mass media have taken over so much of what, in former days, was his rightful territory. By the subjective, questioning nature of his art, his rigorous concern with seeking the truth, his writings are more likely to be subversive than supportive of the status quo.

A comparatively recent way of attracting widespread attention to poetry has been the organisation of national poetry competitions, with tempting money prizes for the winners. Poetry competitions, on a small scale, have been promoted by literary festivals, societies and magazines for many years, but it is only during the past three or four that widely publicised and extravagantly rewarded events have been promoted by leading Sunday newspapers in conjunction with the BBC and other organisations. In 1980 the Poetry Society and the BBC's Radio 3 ran a competition which offered £1,000 as first prize and, at the time of writing, the *Observer*, the Arvon Foundation and the *South Bank Show* have united to launch an even more remunerative competition with no less than £5,000 for the winner. There has been a good deal of controversy, some of it conducted in the correspondence columns of the *Times Literary Supplement*, about the value and desirability, even the morality, of events like these.

The argument in favour of these competitions takes the line that, since all the entries are submitted pseudonymously, the judgement must therefore be entirely objective and an unknown, unpublished writer of talent is just as likely to be chosen as a poet of established reputation. This is partly true. But when the judges are confronted by thousands of manuscripts one wonders how they can confidently decide that one poem is clearly superior to all the others, especially when there has been no restriction regarding subject matter or form. How on earth, for example, comparing pairs of poems by past contemporaries, could anyone say that Wilfred Owen's *Anthem for Doomed Youth* (page 78) is a *better* poem that Edward Thomas's *Thaw* (page 79), or that Shakespeare's sonnet, *That Time of Year . . .* (page 47) is the winner over Donne's *A Valediction: Forbidding Mourning* (page 97)? The truth is that poetry is not a competitive game, and the fact that every writer entering for these events has to pay a fee of £1 or £1–50 for each piece of work submitted, increases my own suspicion that poetry competitions are, in the long run, more harmful than beneficial. The organisers and prizewinners will certainly profit; but the twenty-odd thousand or so also-rans will have little to rejoice over.

I am well aware that unpublished poets feel, sometimes with justification, that their work is as good as much that appears in print above the names of writers of some reputation, and that they believe that the poetry competition offers them a hope, however slender, of gaining not only financial reward but, probably more important, public recognition.

Logically, this would seem to be so, but the odds against even the outstanding poem being selected are immense. The judges, authoritative as they may be, are human, fallible and subject to prejudice, personal predilection, stomach upsets and moments of lack of concentration. The only way, I am sure, for the apprentice poet to make a reputation is the traditional one of sending his work to editors of magazines which specialise in printing poetry and preparing himself for, in most cases, a period of rejection and disappointment. A period of this kind is part of the process of maturing as a writer, and may be seen as a kind of test of seriousness. The writer who is going to stop writing poetry because his work has been rejected by editors is one who has been wrongly motivated in the first place, and one cannot help suspecting that his poems were not rejected without sound critical reason. I believe that, sooner or later, the man or woman who is a dedicated practitioner of the craft and art of poetry and who possesses a true gift will be recognised and published.

The desire to appear in print – passion would not be too strong a word in the case of many unpublished poets – is a perfectly understandable one, but, however powerful the longing, it will not itself produce poetry. The impulse to write must be – and with all true poets I am sure that it is – quite pure, an end in itself. Once the work has been completed, however, it is natural that most authors should wish to see what they have written dignified by print and submitted to the scrutiny of an unknown readership. As I have said, the only practicable way to set about realising this wish is to send the poems to magazines. The writer would be foolish to submit work to a journal which he has not first examined. Merely to discover, from a consultation of the *Writer's and Artist's Yearbook* or some such publication, that a certain magazine publishes verse is not enough. The *kind* of verse printed must be assessed. It would be a waste of time and money, for example, for a writer of free verse, preoccupied with modern urban life, to send poems to a magazine that specialised in rural matters and published verse in traditional forms celebrating the beauties of nature. Most public libraries of any size subscribe to literary magazines which regularly publish poetry, some of which specialise in it. Specialist poetry magazines include the

Poetry Review, the *PN Review* and a host of 'little magazines', about many of which the librarian would have information; some of the best-known journals which regularly publish poems are the *TLS*, the *Listener*, the *New Statesman*, the *Literary Review*, *Encounter*, *Stand*, *Ambit* and the *London Magazine*.

Now for a serious word of warning to any embryonic writer: do not, under any circumstances, be tempted to pay for your work to be published. There flourishes in Britain, and no doubt elsewhere, a thriving line of business known as 'vanity publishing', and the firms involved advertise regularly in the national press stating that they are looking for poems to publish. When innocent and misguided writers send their work to the address supplied – and regrettably they do so in large numbers – they are told that their work has been 'accepted' and will be printed but – and here is the snag – only on condition that they pay for the privilege. In fact these firms 'accept' literally everything that is sent to them, and while they do print them in a book – provided, of course, that they have been paid the not inconsiderable sums demanded – this book is never reviewed or properly distributed, and it is doubtful whether it is even seen by anyone except the hoodwinked contributors. To have been published in one of these 'anthologies' is not only valueless as a step towards public recognition, it is a positive impediment, since anyone with any knowledge of the literary world regards the appearance of a writer in any of these volumes as a guarantee of his or her being unpublishable elsewhere, and as being not only inept but also hopelessly gullible.

The best way for the reader who is unfamiliar with what kinds of poetry are being produced today to discover which type of work and which individual authors are most likely to give pleasure is to obtain a comprehensive anthology which includes poems from the whole, or perhaps the later part, of the twentieth century. There are many such anthologies and a number of them appear in the reading list on page 154. One of the most useful and attractive is *The Oxford Book Of Twentieth-Century English Verse*, chosen by Philip Larkin.

This anthology was criticised quite harshly by some reviewers on its publication in 1973, and almost any knowledgeable reader will object to some of the inclusions and omissions, but it is a wide-ranging and remarkably catholic selection of the verse written between, and including, Thomas Hardy, who died in 1928, and Brian Patten, who was born in 1946. I cannot imagine anyone being unable to find in its pages much to beguile, entertain and move, and it does provide a most useful poetic tour of the past seven decades.

Larkin is himself a poet who works uncompromisingly within the tradition of formal English poetry. He has little patience with the wilder kinds of 'experimental' verse and believes in the virtues of order, intelligence and intelligibility. There have been a few avant-garde experiments in the past two decades – attempts to create 'found poems' by arranging phrases and sentences from public notices, cookery books or technological manuals into verse patterns; 'sound poems' which, with the use of electronic aids, have tried to create a non-verbal poetry; and 'concrete poems' which, either by the use of eccentric typography on the page or actually building models, have tried to emphasise the poetic importance of the visual and tactile – but Larkin, very sensibly in my view, will have little to do with any of these aberrations. However, for those readers who may find his anthology too conservative, there are plenty more available.

The poet and critic D. J. Enright has edited a more up-to-date compilation, *The Oxford Book of Contemporary Verse 1945-1980*, which is designed to offer fairly substantial selections from the work of forty poets who have emerged and developed their gifts during the period indicated by the title. Unlike Larkin in his book, Enright does not limit himself to choosing poets born, or long-domiciled, in Britain; he includes, as well as native British poets, writers from the Commonwealth and America. This makes for a varied and always stimulating selection of poetry and, while well-established British writers like Kingsley Amis, Charles Causley, Roy Fuller, Philip Larkin and Ted Hughes are included, there is excellent work from names that may be less familiar to many British readers, such as James K. Baxter, a New Zealander born in 1926, A. D. Hope, an Australian (b. 1907), and the fine American poets Elizabeth Bishop (1911–1979), John Berryman (1914–1972) and Robert Lowell (1917–1977), to mention only a few of the non-Britons.

The Arts Council of Great Britain publishes annually a substantial volume of poems for which a different editor, or pair of editors, is chosen each year, and contributions to this anthology may be submitted to the Council. These anthologies always include, among the work by well-known writers, a good proportion of poems from unpublished or little-known poets. These compilations have taken over from what were known as the annual PEN (Poets, Essayists and Novelists) anthologies which appeared from 1952 until the early 1970s, and these, at least some of which are to be found in any good public library, provide a useful charting of the progress and trends in post-Second World War poetry.

We are all, as readers, limited in some way by our education, emotional and imaginative preferences, prejudices and so forth. In reading the poetry of our more or less immediate contemporaries, work which posterity has not yet had time to sift, and separate the durable and good from the false and disposable, we should not worry too much about any poetry that yields little in the way of pleasure or edification. If it bores, go on to something that doesn't. The chances are that its failure to make an agreeable or stimulating impact is the fault of the writer, not a result of the reader's lack of sympathy or understanding. As with all the arts, so with poetry, much that is pretentious, ill-conceived and ultimately worthless has, for a time, deceived less discerning critics into believing that it is a new and exciting departure from the prevailing orthodoxies. We should always remember that a steady line of descent exists from the poetry of Chaucer to the present time, and that any form of writing which breaks too abruptly away from that line, and claims to be making a new contribution to the art of verse, owing nothing to the poetry of the past, is almost certain to be the work of a charlatan or a fool. For the truth is that all genuinely experimental work – the poetry of Hopkins, Eliot and Pound for example – has been written by authors steeped in the literature of the past and expert in the theory and practice of all traditional poetic forms. One of the sure ways of deepening your understanding and gaining confidence in your own judgement of poetry is to try writing verse yourself.

I have long believed that the only poetic criticism of real value has come from those who are themselves practitioners of the art. Sir Philip Sidney, Dryden, Pope, Samuel Johnson, Wordsworth, Coleridge, Keats, Shelley, Matthew Arnold, T. S. Eliot, William Empson and I. A. Richards – all of these illuminating and influential critics were fine poets, with the possible exception of Richards who was, nevertheless, a prolific writer of verse. The practice of writing in metre and various stanza forms does facilitate, as no other activity can, insights into the processes and problems of poetic composition; besides which, it may prove to be a fascinating and enjoyable pursuit in itself.

The writing of authentic poetry is, of course, something that cannot be taught, since the qualities required for its making – imagination, vision, passionate sympathy – are innate, but any literate person with a feeling for the music of language can learn to compose competent and pleasing verse. So for those readers who feel that they would like to try their hand at writing verse – and it is perfectly possible that some might discover in themselves a talent for composing something deeper and richer than mere verse – I shall devote the final chapter to an attempt at providing some practical guidelines.

8

WRITING YOUR OWN POETRY

The writing of poetry, as I hope I have shown in this book, is a fundamentally different activity from the writing of prose. As I said in the first chapter, the poet is primarily concerned not with communicating information but with making things happen; he aims not at talking about the emotion that is the starting-point of his poem, but at causing that emotion to be reflected in the sensibility of his reader. He does this by using as few abstractions as possible and by creating verbal images which aim at evoking the mood or feeling he wishes to convey. These images are created by the use of carefully chosen nouns, verbs and adjectives, the deployment of metaphors and similes, and such phonetic devices as alliteration, assonance, dissonance and rhyme. The first thing to practise, then, for anyone who wishes to write poetry, is the knack of communicating abstract feelings and ideas through the presentation of concrete images.

I suggest that you attempt the following exercise. Provide yourself, or persuade someone else to provide you, with a list of emotive abstract nouns such as beauty, rage, love, terror, happiness, loneliness, hatred, peace and so on. Then write a few lines in which you attempt to embody the sense of the abstraction you have chosen, without using the word itself and, ideally, using no abstract nouns at all. At this stage, and assuming that you have had no previous experience at all of verse-writing, I recommend that you should not concern yourself with metre, though in order not to write 'chopped prose' you would do well to fix in your mind's ear a basic rhythm, however loose, and try to incorporate it into your lines. Also, partly in order to introduce a further small element of shaping and control into the exercise, it might prove more interesting and slightly more demanding to make an acrostic on the abstract word selected. For example, choosing the word 'beauty', one might write something like this:

> B lue hills dissolving into
> E vening sky's old velvet,
> A pril dew falling, starring the grass;
> U nder soft covers the fragrant soil
> T rembles with the earth's first
> Y es.

or this

> B lackberries, dew-drenched, wink in green hedges;
> E legant willows make eloquent gestures
> A nd swallows, like skaters, swoop in the blue.
> U nder the oak and the sycamore, shadows
> T hrow down their dark and diaphanous garments.
> Y our heart harbours birds which sing all day
> through.

The first example, by a young student, seems to be a reasonably good start. The second writer has taken a little more care over his use of rhythm, and has used end-rhyme in lines 3 and 6, producing a more conventional piece of verse, though not, for that reason, necessarily a better piece of writing. Here is another sample, this time using 'loneliness' as the abstraction which is to be embodied:

L eft, like a lost glove, in the deserted park
O n the littered, cropped grass,
N o one to notice her, no one to see.
E vening chimes with a faint Angelus,
L ight fades and street lamps in the distance shine.
I n the town friends and lovers are meeting,
N ight will be her sole companion.
E ven the stars turn their faces away from her.
S ilence is swollen not broken by
S igh and murmur of faraway traffic.

Here the writer has not tried to follow any regular pattern of stresses; the verse is free, but there is enough rhythmic regularity for it to escape charges of prosiness.

The imagery in all these attempts is reasonably effective, but nowhere remarkably so. The first example is pleasing but unsurprising; in the second the metaphor of the blackberries winking is agreeable enough, but again it does not have the power to give the reader that little thrill of both surprise and recognition which the best imagery always communicates. Perhaps the solitary woman, the only person in a deserted urban park, being compared with a lost glove is a little more unexpected, and perhaps the sense of loneliness is here better conveyed than the, admittedly more elusive, quality of beauty in the first two.

Another useful exercise which compels the student to express meaning through images is the composition of poetic riddles. The riddle is one of the very oldest of English poetic forms, and the *Exeter Book,* a manuscript collection of Old English poems preserved in the library of Exeter Cathedral since about 1071, contains, among narrative and devotional poetry, eighty-nine examples based upon Latin models. Here is just the beginning of a rough translation from the original Anglo-Saxon of the thirtieth riddle:

I have been a wight wonderfully shaped
Bearing up booty, in between his horns,
A lift-vessel flashing light and bedecked with
loveliness,
Bearing home booty from his war-marching.

The answer to the complete riddle is the new moon with the old moon in its arms. Obviously the maker of riddles must use metaphorical language, the more ingenious the better, though ideally the imagery should be visually accurate and the reader ought, even if he cannot guess the answer, to sense at once the mysterious effectiveness of the metaphors used.

When teaching students on poetry-writing courses, I have suggested that they construct riddles on themes of the following kind: a street lamp, a railway locomotive, a tulip, a telephone, the wind, a horse, a knife, an onion, etc. Again, regular metre is not necessary, though a strong rhythmic base is desirable and rhyme, or near rhyme, may help to convey that sense of the incantatory and mysterious that many of the old Anglo-Saxon riddles communicate. Here are a couple of examples of my students' attempts on themes not included in the list above. See if you can determine what is being described in each riddle before going on to the next paragraph, which supplies the answers.

I have been danced upon beneath the stars;
Fragments of me could be used by murderers.
I have been fashioned by the patient years
Into suspended, glittering chandeliers.
Like you, and all that lives, I too respond
To warmth, become gentle, caressing, fond.
Now I am silent, secretive and still,
Yet once I frolicked on a summer hill.

Shapely the curves, smooth and hard,
Symmetrical and patterned with faint lines
And only when in use can it be heard,
The flattened head the only part that turns.
It is a foreign prince with dusky skin
And tiny metal crown upon his head,
A large brown chess-board piece without a board
And filled with little shrivelled spheres of black
Which, if bitten hard, would bite you back.

The answer to the first riddle is ice, and to the second, a pepper-mill. In each case, I think, the student has provided fair clues and has managed to introduce quite pleasing metaphors. The 'fragments', in line 2 of the first riddle, are the shards of broken ice which could be used, like knife-blades, as murder weapons; the chandeliers, of course, are stalactites, and the reference to frolicking on a summer hill suggests that the ice of the river, or lake, was once a waterfall on the hill-side.

The only reference in the second example that I found at all obscure was the 'patterned with faint lines' which, as the writer explained, described the grain of the wood on the par-ticular pepper-mill she was looking at. While the acrostic and riddle exercises are unlikely to produce poems of real merit, they are both very useful ways of learning how to look hard at the thing being described and to use metaphorical language. They can also be quite fun to produce.

Before proceeding to the use of traditional English metres and verse forms it should prove valuable to spend a lit-tle time over a kind of metre which has been used by a num-ber of British and American poets in the twentieth century, but which is Japanese in origin. Metre in oriental languages does not depend on stress, but on pitch, so the nearest to Japanese verse that poets writing in English can approach is to ignore all the traditional elements of stress in their native prosody and compose in lines containing a predetermined number of syllables, ignoring completely where the accents may fall. This kind of metre is called simply 'syllabics', and the reason why some contemporary poets have used the form is because they have felt that the regularity of the old metrical patterns has become predictable and monotonous, and the device of syllabics provides a way of escaping from the steady pounding of iambs, trochees and the like. The difficulty in using syllabics is that poems composed in this measure do tend to read like 'chopped prose' unless the author has a remarkably sensitive ear.

The most common set forms of syllabic verse are the *haiku* and the *tanka*, both of Japanese origin. The *haiku*, in Japanese, is traditionally a seasonal poem and it follows a fixed pattern: it consists of only three lines, the first of five syll-ables, the second of seven, and the last of five. The first line sets the scene, the second introduces either an actor or an action into the scene, and the last line creates a relationship or fusion between the two. The *haiku* is a picturesque form, like a miniature painting in words, and it deliberately eschews making any comment. The Imagist poets Hulme and Pound were clearly influenced by this form, which they had come across in French translation from the Japanese.

One can compose a kind of westernised *Haiku*, ignoring the constraint of the Japanese formula for setting the scene, introduction of actor or event, and reconciliation of the two, by creating a neat, Imagist description of an incident, object or scene in the prescribed syllabic form of 5, 7, 5. One might, for example, decide to deal with the four seasons in this way:

Spring

Buds' soft explosions,
trumpeting of daffodils;
green resurrection.

Summer

Harsh grass, brown and hazed,
green smell from arched hall of trees;
shade dapples, flutters.

Now, taking these two simply as a formal guide, add your own *haiku* representing autumn and winter and go on to write in the same form on other subjects, for example: a cat or any other animal, the seaside, a Christmas tree, an old tramp, birdsong, fish, wrestlers, flight, combat, etc.

The *tanka* allows a little more elbow-room, for it consists of thirty-one syllables arranged in lines of 5, 7, 5, 7, 7. Here are two examples written by students on a poetry course:

At the Local

In the public house
old men with strong oaken hands
finger dominoes,
small oblong nights of white stars.
We hear the click of cold bones.

From the Cliffs

Grass, white-starred, stops, torn.
Ragged sea winks, diamond-flash.
Paper birds, flung wide,
falter, spiral down, yelping.
Curling blue dissoves to lace.

All the exercises we have so far looked at have the principal purpose of encouraging the writer to think in images and to compress significance within the confines of some kind of form. After you have limbered up and acquired some skill at these you will probably feel ready to attempt something a little more ambitious. Having tried your hand at syllabics, in the form of *haiku* and *tanka,* you should now be ready to experiment with a more flexible use of the technique.

One of the most accomplished exponents of syllabics in the English language is the American poet Marianne Moore, and her use of the form has influenced the work of W. H. Auden and the living British writers Thom Gunn and George MacBeth among others. The whole point of writing in syllabics, as I have pointed out, is to avoid the regularity of orthodox stressed verse. In principle it is a very simple way of composing. All the poet has to do is decide how many syllables are to be used in each line and stick to that pattern, and he need not bother his head about where the stresses fall. In practice, however, he should concern himself with stress in the negative sense of taking pains to *avoid* writing in conventional accented metre. Here is a poem in syllabics by Thom Gunn:

'Blackie, the Electric Rembrandt'

We watch through the shop-front while
Blackie draws stars – an equal

Concentration on his and
The youngster's faces. The hand

is steady and accurate;
but the boy does not see it

for his eyes follow the point
that touches (quick, dark movement!)

a virginal arm beneath
his rolled sleeve: he holds his breath.

. . . Now that it is finished, he
hands a few bills to Blackie

and leaves with a bandage on
his arm, under which gleam ten

stars, hanging in a blue thick
cluster. Now he is starlike.

This is a simple enough and, to my mind, not very impressive piece describing a youth visiting a tattooist somewhere in the United States to have a cluster of stars imprinted on his arm. Every line of the poem contains exactly seven syllables, and it would be a waste of time to try to find any fixed pattern of stresses. The only technical device employed, apart from the syllable count, is the rhyming, or rather the near-rhyming, of each couplet. It is probably a good idea, though by no means obligatory, to use rhyme when writing in syllabics, otherwise the whole thing is likely to turn into something uncomfortably close to prose arranged typographically to look like verse. I have myself used rhyme in the following slight piece (see page 44 for the 'rhyme-pattern borrowed from Alfred, Lord Tennyson' – the *In Memoriam* stanza):

Simplicities

Now that you have gone
I feel a compulsion to write
not literature but something quite
private, for your eyes only to look upon.

It is good, for once,
to ignore the demands of art,
utter simplicities of the heart
and happily become your passionate dunce.

Yet instinct compels
me to accept a formal task;
speech from behind ceremony's mask
might chime with the truth and music of bright bells.

So I have chosen
a syllabic measure this time,
linking these awkward lines with a rhyme-
pattern borrowed from Alfred, Lord Tennyson.

All I wish to do
though is something simple as this:
tell you how I still taste your last kiss,
and say, like any dunce, how much I love you.

In the first stanza I have chosen to vary the number of syllables in each line, though once the order is established it is
strictly followed in the other four stanzas. The syllable count is
as follows: line 1 has five syllables, line 2 has eight, line 3 has
nine (I have counted 'literature' as four syllables, though I am
aware that the word is often pronounced as if it contained
three), and line 4 has eleven. You may notice that, apart from
line 2, each of the other lines contains an odd number of syllables. This was not an arbitrary decision. If the writer chooses
to make his lines of eight or ten syllables he is far more likely
to fall into the regular metrical rhythm of the iambic tetrameter and pentameter (see Chapter 3).

Should you feel like trying syllabics as an exercise you
may set out your poem on the page in any way you wish.
There is no need to arrange the lines in couplets, quatrains or
any kind of set pattern; decide which graphic arrangement is
the most aesthetically pleasing to you, and set your poem
down in that way. Syllabics – lacking the greater formality of
accented metrical verse, with or without rhyme – is a suitable
measure for subjects which lend themselves to a fairly
relaxed, conversational or ruminative style. *Simplicities* tries
to capture and preserve that afterglow of pleasure and affection which attends the departure of one's beloved and, by
imposing upon itself the order of syllabics, it suggests that,
however spontaneous and intimate the impulse to speak
about the heart's affections, effective utterance requires some
kind of shaping, preferably that of art. Nevertheless the poem
is trying to simulate the casual, almost random, nature of idle
reflection.

If you have no immediate ideas or feelings that might

provide subjects which could be appropriately realised in syllabics, I suggest you attempt the following exercise: compose,
in syllabics, a mock Last Will and Testament. This notion
posesses, among other possibilities, a capacity for effective
satire: you could feature in your verses either public figures or
private acquaintances. For instance, if your political views
were of a radical kind, you might choose to be beastly to the
Prime Minister:

My last Will and Testament:	7
I, John Smith, bequeath	5
a sense of social justice	7
and Gladstonian whiskers	7
to Mrs Thatcher.	5

Using this stanza as a matrix for the syllabic line length you
could proceed to celebrities in other fields of endeavour. For
example:

> To the Poet Laureate
> a Victorian
> chamber pot, a new felt hat,
> a rhyming dictionary
> and a teddy bear.
>
> To Mr Frank Sinatra
> some self-effacement,
> a final final concert,
> some pomade, a brush and comb
> and natural hair.

Of course syllabics can be and have been used for much more
serious purposes. W. H. Auden has written a fine poem using
the form, *In Memory of Sigmund Freud*. Here are the first
eleven stanzas:

> When there are so many we shall have to mourn,
> when grief has been made so public, and exposed
> to the critique of a whole epoch
> the frailty of our conscience and anguish,

of whom shall we speak? For every day they die
among us, those who were doing us some good,
      who knew it was never enough but
    hoped to improve a little by living.

Such was this doctor: still at eighty he wished
to think of our life from whose unruliness
      so many plausible young futures
    with threats of flattery ask obedience,

but his wish was denied him: he closed his eyes
upon that last picture, common to us all,
      of problems like relatives gathered
    puzzled and jealous about our dying.

For about him till the very end were still
those he had studied, the fauna of the night,
      and shades that still waited to enter
    the bright circle of his recognition

turned elsewhere with their disappointment as he was
taken away from his life interest
      to go back to the earth in London
    an important Jew who died in exile.

Only Hate was happy, hoping to augment
his practice now, and his dingy clientele
      who think they can be cured by killing
    and covering the gardens with ashes.

They are still alive, but in a world he changed
simply by looking back with no false regrets;
      all he did was to remember
    like the old and be honest like children.

He wasn't clever at all: he merely told
the unhappy Present to recite the Past
      like a poetry lesson till sooner
    or later it faltered at the line where

long ago the accusations had begun,
and suddenly knew by whom it had been judged,
      how rich life had been and how silly,
    and was life-forgiven and more humble,

able to approach the Future as a friend
without a wardrobe of excuses, without
      a set mask of rectitude or an
    embarrassing over-familiar gesture.

There are another seventeen stanzas of this admirable poem, and careful study of Auden's technique should be valuable in showing how syllabics can sustain a contemplative note of gravity appropriate to the subject, and present both a moving tribute to, and shrewd assessment of, the great analyst's achievement. The syllabic pattern for each stanza is 11, 11, 9, 10 and rhyme is deliberately avoided. Obviously the use of syllabics is limited to a certain type of subject matter, and could not accommodate lyricism.

The next verse form to practise is iambic pentameter (see Chapter 3), and before attempting to incorporate rhyme I think it would be wise to master writing blank verse. This measure is suited to almost any kind of theme. You could decide to adopt a dramatic persona, in the manner of Robert Browning, imagining that you are a character in history or a fictional personage delivering a speech from a play. Or you could simply write a passage of description, taking any landscape, urban or rural, as your subject. Blank verse can be used, too, for telling a story. A rewarding exercise can be performed by taking a familiar tale from Greek mythology, the Bible or history and recasting it in blank verse, making as much use as possible of striking imagery.

Until now we have been dealing with more or less mechanical exercises and it is time for me to make a very important point. In the writing of a real poem it is very rare for the author to complete the work at a single attempt. The most usual way for a poet to work is as follows: first, the idea, experience or original mood forms in his consciousness. He will then write down the images that he hopes to develop, not worrying at this stage about formal considerations. When he has completed this, his first draft, it will almost certainly be without structural or logical coherence, but there will probably be at least a few phrases, even whole lines, that will appear in the finished work. Next comes the business of ordering the rough primary outline into a harmonious pattern, and in this process it frequently happens that some of the original images and ideas will be discarded and others will replace them. It is by no means an uncommon occurrence for a poet to construct many drafts before he arrives at the fully realised poem.

I hope it will prove instructive if I take a poem by a young student and show the stages through which it progressed to its final form. The student, a girl of twenty, had not attempted to write poetry before and possessed little, if any, knowledge of poetic technique. What follows now is a replica of her first draft:

> A fly walks up the window
> behind the fly the trees wave
> a group of stately and proud women
> their undergowns turning gold
> in the dying autumn sun
> The rustle of their skirts
> almost hidden by the music
> inside the room pouring out
> plinkety-plunkety notes
> weaving their pattern of darkness and light
> click! the music is finished
> and leaves the air blank
> but the women outside
> still dance

When I was shown this I made a few suggestions, simply about the choice of language, and the student went away to write a second draft, returning with this:

> A fly moves aimlessly up the window-pane
> through the glass the trees wave
> A group of stately dowagers and daughters
> their undergowns turning russet and gold
> in the autumnal light
> The rustle of their skirts almost hidden
> by the music inside the room
> pouring out quill-plucked notes
> weaving its pattern of light and dark
>
> The record is suddenly stopped
> leaving the air blank
> but the women outside still dance.

Here 'moves' has been substituted for 'walks', and while the substituted word is imprecise it is undoubtedly an improvement, because 'walks' possesses strong human associations, suggesting striding, tramping, marching, strolling, ambling, all decidedly unsuitable for the movement of a fly. We find the more carefully observed adjective 'russet' applied to the gowns, or leaves, and the substitution of 'quill-plucked' for the disastrously whimsical 'plinkety-plunkety', and so on.

The second version is marginally more pleasing than the first, but still in need of a good deal of revision before it could claim to be called, in its modest way, a poem. At this point I suggested that she should impose on it the order of regular metre, and it seemed – taking into consideration her lack of experience in verse-writing and the nature of the poem – that blank verse would be the most suitable form. The student did not know what blank verse constituted, so I spent a little time explaining the nature of an iambic pentameter and gave her the first line of Gray's *Elegy Written in a Country Churchyard* as a model. I also suggested that perhaps the presence of the fly was superfluous. Off she went to recast her poem into blank verse, and after some effort produced this:

> The light is fading as the music plays,
> The quill-plucked notes strung out on silence
> Gleam in fragile clusters in the room.
> Beyond transforming glass the towering trees
> Perform their gracious sarabande;
> Stately dowagers chaperone their young;
> Their undergowns are turning russet, gold;
> The whisper of autumnal skirts intrudes
> Its ceaseless rustle underneath the rich
> Harmonies that almost drown its speech,
> And bring into this room a former age.
>
> The record moves towards its end. A click.
> The air is blank. The past recedes, and yet
> Outside, the women still compose their dance.

Now the piece began to feel and sound much more like a poem. We noticed, on reading it through, that lines 2 and 5 were each short of a stress and, though I did not think this mattered very much, the student was determined to have her work at least technically correct, so she prepared a final version:

An Autumn Dance

The light is fading as the music plays;
Its quill-plucked, plangent notes strung out on silence
Gleam in fragile clusters in the room.
Beyond transforming glass the towering trees
Perform a green and gracious sarabande;
Stately dowagers chaperone their young;
Their undergowns are turning russet, gold;
The sweeping of autumnal skirts intrudes
Its ceaseless whisper underneath the rich
Harmonies that almost drown its speech.
The record moves towards its end. A click.
The air is blank, the past recedes, and yet
Outside, the dance, the endless dance.

The last line of this is one foot short of a regular pentameter but the author, who was well aware of this, felt that her new ending was more effective that way and she, of course, was the final arbiter.

I have spent rather a lot of time and space on the evolution of one student's poem because I believe that it does show conclusively how, by focusing attention on every word and subjecting the rush of spontaneous feeling and images to the rein of formal verse, a negligible piece of writing can be turned into something quite respectable. The student who wrote *An Autumn Dance* has since progressed to writing far more impressive poems.

Before going further I suggest that you turn back to Chapter 3 to read the section on rhyme and stanza forms. You should then be ready to experiment with some of these devices. The use of rhyme is often thought of by inexperienced writers as severely restrictive, but in fact it need not be nearly so inhibiting as at first it might seem. Rhyme not only creates pleasing auditory effects but it can actually be productive of ideas, and even images, which might not have come to the poet had he not been using the device. By this I mean that it quite often happens that, in the search for a rhyming word, an author will strike on one which suggests an unexpected and felicitous metaphor or a fresh direction for his poem to take, and as a consequence his work may be enriched. The danger, especially with unpractised writers, is that the search for an elusive rhyme may force him into introducing material that he does *not* want in his poem, or he may feel compelled to torture syntax in order to achieve an end rhyme. If you find that you can think of no suitable rhyming word it may be necessary to go back to the line whose last word demands the echo, and change it for a word of similar meaning and associations. This, too, rarely harms the completed poem and may frequently improve it.

Rhyme may be used not only for creating a pleasant effect of euphony, but, because end rhymes draw attention to themselves, they can also focus the reader's attention on key words. In this lyric by Shelley we can see how the rhyming words are linked not merely by the end sounds but also by meaning and association. 'Overpast' and 'last' are related by antithesis or opposition; 'keep' and 'deep' are mutually strengthening but are then opposed by 'weep'. 'See' and 'tenderly' support each other, 'be' is modified by 'unseen' and the past participle, 'been' sounds a note of the irrevocably lost. And so on.

To

I

When passion's trance is overpast,
If tenderness and truth could last,
Or live, whilst all wild feelings keep
Some mortal slumber, dark and deep,
I should not weep, I should not weep!

II

It were enough to feel, to see,
Thy soft eyes gazing tenderly,
And dream the rest – and burn and be
The secret food of fires unseen,
Couldst thou but be as thou hast been.

III

After the slumber of the year
The woodland violets reappear;
All things revive in field or grove,
A sky and sea, but two, which move
And form all others, life and love,

To return now to practical work: I take it that by now you have had experience in using the pentameter, so you should be equipped to attempt a sonnet. The exercise I am about to suggest has its disadvantages: it cannot, even by divine accident, produce a genuine poem, and on no account must the student believe that anything of true literary worth can be produced in this way. However it has its uses, too, and so long as you treat it simply as further practice in writing in metre it will serve its purpose and you will have the satisfaction of having produced something resembling a sonnet.

This exercise consists in someone supplying, or you yourself supplying, fourteen words which will follow the rhyme scheme of a Petrarchan or English sonnet. These are set down on the page as the end line words, and you are then required to fill up the lines in the correct metre, iambic pentameters. At a poetry workshop I set students the following pattern of words, conforming to the scheme of the English sonnet: sky, gold, defy, cold, trees, trail, freeze, hail, arms, yearn, farms, turn, reach, speech. The following is fairly representative of the exercises produced:

> The eastern sun has stained the wounded *sky*
> With streaks of blood and counterpoint of *gold;*
> The urban concrete boxes may *defy*
> The depredations of the ruthless *cold,*
> But far beyond the town, among the *trees*
> And icy fields, the season leaves its *trail*
> Of vanquished victims who must lie and *freeze*
> Until, insensible to frost and *hail*
> They have laid down their lives and useless *arms.*
> They will not dream of peaceful homes nor *yearn*
> Again for simple pleasures, summer *farms,*
> The skies of infancy. Not one may *turn*
> Again in his white endless sleep to *reach*
> For body's warmth or soft, consoling *speech.*

Considering the circumstances of its composition it is a creditable piece of work, but I should prefer to see students using the rhyme pattern creatively, choosing their own themes and, of course, not pre-selecting the rhyming words.

Much less demanding, indeed probably the simplest

of all rhyming stanzas, is the ballad form. As we have seen in Chapter 4, the simplest ballad stanza, that used in *Sir Patrick Spens*, consists of quatrains of tetrameters and trimeters rhyming ABCB, but you can, if you wish, elaborate on this basic pattern. Old as the ballad is as a literary form, it is still very much alive and splendid effects, both comic and serious, can be achieved within its compass. It is an ideal form for the retelling of folk stories as well as for new, perhaps cautionary, tales. To see what the modern ballad can achieve turn back to *The Ballad of the Faithless Wife* (Chapter 4) and seek out W. H. Auden's *Miss Gee, Victor* and *As I Walked Out One Evening.* For themes you might choose from history, recent or ancient, topical events, fantasy or anything that lends itself to direct narrative treatment.

When you have tried your hand at the sonnet and ballad you may feel like writing in some of the other metres and stanza forms described in Chapter 3. Fluency in, for example, rhymed couplets may be gained simply by setting yourself a subject and writing in that form or by taking a passage of prose and either recasting it into verse; alternatively, and better, using it as a starting-point, paraphrase or play variations upon it. If you choose to do the latter it will be necessary to find a suitably thoughtful and fairly rhetorical passage, an essay by Lamb or Hazlitt perhaps, or a few paragraphs of description from Dickens.

If you should belong to, or decide to form, a small circle of friends who are interested in writing verse various entertaining literary games can be played which have the quite serious purpose of increasing the facility with which you handle metre and rhyme. For a collaborative making of rhymed couplets you need only one partner. One person writes a rhymed couplet on any theme, then he or she adds a third line which is, of course, unrhyming. These three lines are handed to the partner who then adds a line which rhymes with the last one given, and adds a fourth, unrhyming, one to give back to the writer of the first line. From then on, to the end or collapse of the poem, each writer alternately adds two lines, the first one, of course, having to rhyme with the preceding line and the second ending with a word for which the partner must find a rhyme.

Another verbal game, preferably engaging four or five people, is played as follows: each participant has a sheet of paper which he divides into a number of columns. The columns may be headed thus – Adjective/Noun/Verb/Adverb/ Noun/Verb/Adverb/Noun – or any combination of these parts of speech that will make an interesting sentence. If there are five participants each person writes down five adjectives in the first column. The paper is then folded back, so that the words cannot be seen, and each sheet is passed to the player on the right. Now five nouns are written down, the paper folded back again and passed on; five verbs, adverbs and so on until all the columns have been filled. The pages are then opened out and the players may add prepositions, conjunctions, definite and indefinite articles; they may pluralise the nouns and, if they wish, change the tenses of the verbs, but they cannot alter the order of the five key words. The object is to try to make a five-lined 'poem'. The results can be strange, sometimes absurd, but surprisingly often lines of mysterious beauty or fecund mystery emerge.

You may well be wondering what a game of this kind has to do with writing poetry. For one thing it can show how the yoking of quite unrelated concepts sometimes produces images of disturbing power. It can also demonstrate the fact that there is often an element of chance in the making of poetically effective phrases. There is another group game of a rather similar kind which serves the same purpose, besides being fascinating to play. This one, however, does involve less pure chance and is a far more creative exercise.

Each member writes ten lines of original verse on any theme, though light or comic verse should be firmly ruled out. While there is no rigid stipulation as to metre or the use of rhyme, it should be suggested that the lines are of reasonable length, four or five stresses, or eight to eleven syllables, would seem the most practicable. When the lines have been composed each writer should copy them out in clear block capitals, leaving a generous space between each line. All the verses are then cut up with scissors into separate lines. If there are five people involved the fifty lines are put into some kind of receptacle, a waste-paper basket for example, and well shaken up. Then each person takes out ten lines – obviously it is unlikely that he will get back more than one or two of his own composition. The final stage is to arrange these lines into a coherent pattern, hoping that something like a poem will emerge. To make this more likely four fresh original lines may be added, not necessarily consecutively, at any point in the poem.

I have conducted this poetry game on many occasions and almost invariably something of interest is produced. The following lines are the result of one such game and, while they may not amount to a poem of very great merit, and their total meaning is, to say the least, rather obscure, it is by no means a derisory piece of writing. What commends this game or exercise is that it is enjoyable to do and it does involve the inventive use of language. Furthermore, like the other group game, it points towards that indefinable mystery that is part of poetry's fascination:

> Knife-blades through the shifting mass of
> bouldering cloud,
> That here display their massive grief,
> Bluster against the venomously gentle,
> Deny their mortal import, are luminous and kind.
> Such contradictions are the stuff of hope.
> How strange to find one feels so strongly for
> The self-effacing trivia of our days.
> What does it matter if a child should cry,
> That the words of love fade on the jaundiced page?
> The night is full of time enough to die,
> To prove the hoped-for consummation true,
> Subjection that will offer more than peace.

I hope that you have not found this final chapter too schoolmasterly in tone and – though this may sound contradictory – too much concerned with trivialities, party games and the like. The reader who is interested in trying to write poetry will, it is hoped, be able to develop his own variations on the different exercises I have outlined and acquire some skill in using language with something of the formality that poetry demands. Until he has learnt that versification is a fairly complex art, and has mastered at least a few of the principles on which it is based, he will not be equipped to tackle the job of transmuting his raw experience into art.

Of course, authentic poetry cannot be written to a pre-scription or formula, but the groundwork must first be done. I can think of no poet who was not thoroughly practised in the mechanics of his craft before he was able to produce work of distinction. The notion of the blazing young genius who exudes his inspired lyrics like ectoplasm is simply not sup-ported by historical fact. Some of the poets themselves have been partly responsible for this fiction. Pope's words in his *Epistle to Dr Arbuthnot,*

> As yet a child, nor yet a fool to fame,
> I lisped in numbers, for the numbers came. . .

tell us, with perfect truth, that the poet displayed an extra-ordinarily precocious talent for verse. 'Numbers' here means poetic metre. Pope's youthful writing was remarkably accom-plished, but there was no question of his skill being purely instinctive. Of course he possessed unusual natural gifts of intelligence and imagination, but the quality of his juvenilia was the result of hard study in the techniques of his masters, in the classical languages as well as in English poetry. He wrote this at the age of thirteen:

Of a Lady Singing to her Lute

Fair charmer cease, nor make your voice's prize
A heart resign'd the conquest of your eyes:
Well might, alas! that threaten'd vessel fail,
Which winds and lightning both at once assail.
We were too blest with these inchanting lays,
Which must be heav'nly when an angel plays;
But killing charms your lover's death contrive,
Lest heav'nly musick should be heard alive.
Orpheus could charm the trees, but thus a tree
Taught by your hand, can charm no less than he;
A poet made the silent wood pursue;
This vocal wood had drawn the poet too.

As the poet himself states, this ingenious and delightful piece of work is an imitation of the style of Edmund Waller. Between the ages of twelve and fifteen Pope set himself the task of writ-ing poems in the manner of Chaucer, Spenser, Waller and

Cowley and in making translations or 'imitations', from the French of Malherbe and the Latin of St Francis Xavier, Tibullus, Martial and others. The young John Keats, a century later, made his imitations of Spenser, Milton and Shakespeare before he discovered his own individual tone of voice. In our own century Dylan Thomas, who wrote wonderfully original poems in his quite early teens and whom the ill-informed have tried to erect as the image of wild, untutored genius, was the son of a poetry-loving schoolmaster and was absorbing Shakespeare, Blake and Tennyson at an age when most children have scarcely progressed beyond comic papers.

The imitation of great poets whom you admire is clearly a practice that can be rewarding. As long as your models are excellent nothing but good can come of it. But it is only a start. Most young poets begin by being delighted and moved by the poetry they have read. They say to themselves, 'That is what I want to do! What greater joy could I hope to gain than write a poem like one of Shakespeare's sonnets, a Donne love poem, a Tennyson lyric, a Dylan Thomas incantation.' Attempts to write in the manner of any, or all, of these poets may well be of help to the apprentice; he will acquire skills in the handling of different metres, stanza forms, styles. He will learn to search for the exact word and combination of words which satisfy the ear, the intelligence and the imagination. He will discover something of the potential power of metaphor. But, if he is to become an authentic poet and not merely a clever fabricator of pastiche, he will reach the revelatory stage at which he will be struck by this crucial realisation: he must, when writing his own poems, forget all that has been written by other poets. He will have learnt all in the way of fundamental technique that he needs to learn from his masters; now is the time for him to concentrate his entire resources, intellectual, imaginative and emotional, on the problem of exploring the experiences from which he wishes to take his poems and strive uncompromisingly to tell the truth about them. It is in this way that a true poet finds his own unique voice.

A mastery of the craft of verse is essential for the person who is to write real poems, but this alone is not enough. There are many writers who are immensely skilled verse technicians but who have never written a true poem. I believe that the genuine poem proceeds from the imagination, the clear vision and, above all, the determination not to falsify your own emotional responses. You must not attempt to squeeze more emotional juice from the experience you are dealing with than it naturally contains. You must tell the truth.

Poems, as I hope we have seen, can be about any subject whatsoever. The essential factor is that the experience, whether it is a deeply personal one – a love affair, a hate affair, a bereavement, a religious conversion, a loss of faith, involvement in disaster or triumph – or a simple response to something observed – a landscape, person, animal, or machine – must be one that has genuinely moved you and rooted itself hauntingly in your imaginative consciousness. Through regularly writing poems one develops the habit of vigilance, of constantly being on the look-out for possible poems or images that might find their place in poems. A street accident, to the poet, is not simply a shocking event to be forgotten as quickly as possible. It is the seed of a potential poem. A walk on the beach or in a secluded wood is not only an enjoyable way of passing the time; it might yield sensations and images which will be preserved in the aspic of verse. The poet celebrates, commemorates, laments, affirms, or attacks: he seizes upon the temporal, the transitory, and fixes it in language for the attention and possible consolation or delight of posterity.

It is a good idea to carry with you a small notebook in which you can jot down those fugitive images, feelings and ideas that might otherwise escape into oblivion. Above all it is necessary for the man or woman who wishes to write real poetry to be saturated in the stuff. Read widely, from all periods, and listen to it being spoken on gramophone records, on the radio and at public recitals. Whether or not you ever produce a poem of great distinction yourself – splendid though this would be for you – it is less important than the fact that your life will, I firmly believe, be immeasurably enriched by your experience of reading, and perhaps trying to write, poetry.

recommended further reading

I have deliberately restricted the number of books in this list to those which I believe should prove especially enjoyable and useful. Details of collections by individual poets may be obtained from any good bookshop or public library, and I hope that the reader will be stimulated to go on to the collected works of those poets he encountered and particularly enjoyed in the recommended anthologies.

anthologies

The London Book of English Verse, ed. Read and Bobrée.
  Eyre Methuen

Poets of the English Language (5 vols),
  ed. Auden and Holmes Pearson. Eyre Methuen

The Poet's Tongue, ed. Auden and Garrett. Bell

The Oxford Book of Modern Verse 1892–1935,
  chosen by W. B. Yeats. OUP

The New Oxford Book of English Verse,
  ed. Helen Gardner. OUP

The Oxford Book of English Verse, ed. Quiller-Couch. OUP

The Oxford Book of Ballads, ed. James Kinsley. OUP

The Oxford Book of American Verse,
  chosen by F. O. Matthiessen. OUP

The New Oxford Book of American Verse,
  ed. Richard Ellmann. OUP

The Oxford Book of Twentieth-Century English Verse,
  chosen by Philip Larkin. OUP

The Oxford Book of Contemporary Verse 1945–1980,
  chosen by D. J. Enright. OUP

The Albatross Book of Living Verse,
  ed. Louis Untermeyer. Collins

The Penguin Book of English Verse,
  ed. John Hayward. Penguin

The Penguin Book of Contemporary American Poetry,
  ed. Donald Hall. Penguin

The Penguin Modern Poets (series)

Longer Contemporary Poems, ed. David Wright. Penguin

New Lines 1 and 2, ed. Robert Conquest. Macmillan

Love, ed. de la Mare. Faber

Come Hither, ed. de la Mare. Faber

Behold This Dreamer, ed. de la Mare. Faber

A Flock of Words, ed. Mackay. Bodley Head

The Terrible Rain (The War Poets 1939–1945),
  ed. Brian Gardner. Eyre Methuen

The Poetry of War, ed. Ian Hamilton. New English Library

criticism

The New Poetic, C. K. Stead. Hutchinson

Image and Experience, Graham Hough. Duckworth

Poetry and the Age, Randall Jarrell. Faber

The Dyer's Hand, W. H. Auden. Faber

Forewords and Afterwords, W. H. Auden. Faber

Practical Criticism, I. A. Richards. Routledge

ABC of Reading, Ezra Pound. Faber

Twentieth-Century Poetry, ed. Martin and Furbank.
  Open University Press

practical

Does it Have to Rhyme? Sandy Brownjohn. Hodder & Stoughton
What Rhymes with Secret? Sandy Brownjohn. Hodder & Stoughton

index

acknowledgements

For permission to reprint copyright material, the publishers gratefully acknowledge the following:

Faber & Faber Ltd for 'Gare du Midi', 'Who's Who', 'Night Mail' and 'In Memory of Sigmund Freud' from *Collected Poems* by W. H. Auden; David Higham Associates for 'Ballad of the Faithless Wife' from *Collected Poems* by Charles Causley, published by Macmillan; Faber & Faber Ltd for 'The Love Song of J. Alfred Prufrock' from *Collected Poems 1909–1962* by T. S. Eliot; the author for 'Xmas for the Boys' (from *Penguin Modern Poets 25*) by Gavin Ewart; the author for 'Black' from *Collected Poems* by Robert Graves; Faber & Faber Ltd for 'Blackie, the Electric Rembrandt' from *My Sad Captains* by Thom Gunn; Faber & Faber Ltd for 'Mr Bleaney' from *The Whitsun Weddings* by Philip Larkin, and 'Sunday Morning' from *The Collected Poems of Wallace Stevens*; David Higham Associates for 'Do not go gentle into that good night' and 'And death shall have no dominion', both from *Collected Poems* by Dylan Thomas, published by J. M. Dent.